A.R.E. MEMBERSHIP SERIES

THE GREAT TEACHINGS OF EDGAR CAYCE

by Mark A. Thurston, Ph.D.,
and the
Editors of the A.R.E.

ASSOCIATION FOR
RESEARCH AND
ENLIGHTENMENT

A.R.E. Press • Virginia Beach • Virginia

A.R.E. Press
Sixty-Eighth & Atlantic Avenue
P.O. Box 656
Virginia Beach, VA 23451-0656

Thurston, Mark A., 1950-
    The great teachings of Edgar Cayce / by Mark A. Thurston
and the editors of the A.R.E.
        p.   cm. (The A.R.E. membership series ; 2)
    ISBN 0-87604-360-0
    1. Cayce, Edgar, 1877-1945.—Edgar Cayce readings. 2. Para-
psychology. 3. Occultism. I. Cayce, Edgar, 1877-1945. Edgar
Cayce readings. Selections. II. Association for Research and
Enlightenment. III. Title. IV. Series.
BP605.A77T48   1996
133.8—dc20   96-7878

THE
GREAT
TEACHINGS OF
EDGAR CAYCE

Contents

The A.R.E. Membership Series:

Edgar Cayce's Approach to Rejuvenation of the Body
The Great Teachings of Edgar Cayce

Introduction

Selecting the finest work of a creative genius is a difficult and subjective task. For example, it's virtually impossible to get consensus on the greatest compositions of Mozart or the best paintings of Monet. The same problem arises in trying to identify the greatest psychic discourses of Edgar Cayce.

As a student of this material for thirty years, I certainly have personal favorites from among the 14,306 choices—readings that have spoken profoundly to my own challenges and needs for understanding. However, in selecting one reading every other month for my "Great Readings" column of *Venture Inward* magazine, I've tried for the last seven years to use a broader criterion: Which teachings from Cayce's psychic discourses address most powerfully the general human condition—issues with which we all wrestle?

For anyone who studies the material carefully, it's an inescapable fact that some Cayce readings are more profound than others. The variability in quality is sometimes related to the sincerity of the seeker or the care with which the questions were formulated. In other cases, though, it seems evident that Cayce himself was more highly attuned to spiritual forces on certain days.

There are thousands of "good readings"—solid, insightful advice—each of them a little miracle in itself if we stop to consider just how extraordinary it is to demonstrate clairvoyance in the first place. But several hundred readings seem to stand out because of their special lucidity, their spiritual power, or the depth of their wisdom on a universal subject. No two experienced students of the Cayce material are likely to agree entirely on which readings fit this category, but all will readily admit that certain teachings deserve special attention.

In this book I've assembled fifteen of these Great Readings. It wasn't an easy task, and the selection process immediately called forth the need for a second volume or more. Each verbatim reading is preceded by my interpretive commentary, an attempt to feature some of the highlights of the reading and offer explanatory ideas. They are grouped into four sections and present a powerful picture of Cayce's central ideas and teachings on four themes. Later volumes of this kind will be able to feature other important themes.

Of course, what ultimately makes a Cayce teaching great is the *application* of the reader—yourself. I hope that in these fifteen special readings and the commentaries I've added you'll find principles and insights which can make a practical difference in the way you live.

Mark Thurston
July 1996

Chapter 1

PHILOSOPHY

READING 5749-14

This is arguably one of *the* most significant readings ever given by Cayce.

It formed the basis of the "Philosophy" chapter in Tom Sugrue's authorized biography of Cayce, *There Is a River.* That chapter offers a systematic summary of the soul's nature and its long journey in the universe. For nearly fifty years that remarkable biography has introduced Cayce's work to hundreds of thousands of people. The "Philosophy" chapter offered the essential foundation for beginning to work with the ideas in the readings. Sugrue probably wouldn't have been able to write it without this reading.

Once you've studied this reading carefully, you might read (or re-read) the "Philosophy" chapter near the end of *There Is a River.* No doubt you'll recognize points that are clearly articulated in this reading. But in other passages from the book, you'll notice that Sugrue had to interpret what he understood from reading 5749-14 and then add to it. It's an especially fine illustration of the process authors try to follow as they take material from the readings and translate it into narratives that make the ideas understandable to general readers.

The first thing that one is likely to notice upon scanning this reading is that some of the two dozen questions take an unusual form. Sugrue had clearly done his homework. He had studied the readings carefully, along with biblical and other philosophical sources. For most of the eleven "problems" (i.e., key issues that Sugrue hoped to clarify for his readers) he had already tried to formulate his own best thinking on the matter, offering Cayce a possible solution and requesting comment. This is a sound strategy, consistent with the approach the readings often encouraged for consulting psychic sources.

Although there are many subtleties and interesting nuances in this reading, at least these five major themes are addressed:

- Creation and the purpose of life
- The importance of free will
- A cosmic view of the soul's journey
- The process of incarnation and influences that shape a lifetime
- The mysteries of Jesus, the Christ

There are, of course, other readings on creation, and Sugrue was able to draw upon them as well. But in this reading, we find an especially straightforward description of the fall of humanity. Cayce takes evil seriously. But to answer the ancient problem of its origins, he focuses on the misuse of free will by souls. To decipher essential points in this portion of the reading, it may be helpful to notice that the term *soul* is used for the spiritual component of our nature, whereas *man* refers to the physical creation that happened much later.

Were souls meant to come to Earth? Here the answer is a little more cryptic ("The earth [was] . . . *not necessarily* as a place of tenancy for the souls of men" [emphasis added]). Apparently it became a place for meaningful experience once souls had created for themselves a fallen condition from the misuse of free will.

In fact, the issue of free will is so prominent throughout this reading that it might well be considered Cayce's most important statement on the subject. The will, one of the three attributes of the soul along with mind and spirit, is described in a variety of ways:

- The cause of the Fall
- The greatest factor (surpassing both heredity and environment) in assisting or hurting soul growth
- The agent by which souls make use of opportunities found in their birth circumstances
- The awakener of the Christ Consciousness resident in the unconscious mind of every soul

Another particularly significant portion of this reading concerns the distinction between Jesus and the Christ. In other readings we can find the idea that "Jesus is the pattern" but that the "power is in the Christ." Here the mission of the soul we know as Jesus is clarified. But Cayce's answer to the question regarding past lives of Jesus/Christ may leave us as bewildered as ever about the distinction. The very wording of Sugrue's question initiates the dilemma: he seems to request previous incarnations of the Christ, as opposed to those of Jesus. Does Cayce's response mean that the being of the Christ had incarnations (i.e., Enoch and Melchizedek) that had nothing to do with the sequence of a soul that became Jesus? Or, does the sequence that includes Joseph, Joshua, Jeshua, and Jesus simply denote a new phase of the same soul's development? We can't be sure—it's open to interpretation.

The final question-and-answer exchange may seem like a request from Sugrue for *personal* advice. Up to this point, the Cayce source has given a thoughtful dissertation on metaphysics—a clairvoyant view of the structure of the universe and human history. Now comes a twist. Cayce adds a moral dimension. Don't try to "go around the Cross." In other words, there's no real understanding of all these matters—creation, Arcturus, the past lives of Jesus, or anything else—unless one also embraces the meaning of self-sacrifice.

The passage might remind us of Gandhi's famous warning: "Be on guard against science without humanity, politics without principle, knowledge without character, wealth without work, commerce without morality, pleasure without consciousness, and worship without sacrifice."

Cayce seems to be speaking in the same spirit. Be on guard about collecting knowledge of higher matters unless you also have the will and ideal to put them into application. Be on guard about exploring the mysteries of metaphysical philosophy and transpersonal psychology unless you're ready to surrender your own agenda and sacrifice your own limited goals in living. That's the most telling summary of Cayce's or any authentic spiritual philosophy.

THE READING

This psychic reading, 5749-14, was given on May 14, 1941, at the request of Thomas Sugrue. The conductor was Hugh Lynn Cayce.

[1]HLC: You will have before you the inquiring mind of the entity, Thomas Sugrue, present in this room, and certain of the problems which confront him in composing the manuscript of *There Is a River*.

The entity is now ready to describe the philosophical concepts which have been given through this source, and wishes to parallel and align them with known religious tenets, especially those of Christian theology. The entity does not wish to set forth a system of thought, nor imply that all questions of a philosophical nature can be answered through this source—the limitations of the finite mind prevent this.

But the entity wishes to answer those questions which will naturally arise in the mind of the reader, and many of the questions which are being asked by all people in the world today.

Therefore the entity presents certain problems and questions, which you will answer as befits the entity's understanding and the task of interpretation before him.

[2]EC: Yes, we have the inquiring mind, Thomas Sugrue, and those problems, those questions that arise in the mind of the entity at this period. Ready for questions.

[3](Q) The first problem concerns the reason for creation. Should this be given as God's desire to experience Himself, God's desire for companionship, God's desire for expression, or in some other way?

(A) God's desire for companionship and expression.

[4](Q) The second problem concerns that which is variously called evil, darkness, negation, sin. Should it be said that this condition existed as a necessary element of creation, and the soul, given free will, found itself with the power to indulge in it, or lose itself in it? Or should it be said that this is a condition created by the activity of the soul itself? Should it be described, in either case, as a state of consciousness, a gradual lack of awareness of self and self's relation to God?

(A) It is the free will and its losing itself in its relationship to God.

[5](Q) The third problem has to do with the fall of man. Should this be described as something which was inevitable in the destiny of souls, or something which God did not desire, but which He did not prevent once He had given free will? The problem here is to reconcile the omniscience of God and His knowledge of all things with the free will of the soul and the soul's fall from grace.

(A) He did not prevent, once having given free will. For,

He made the individual entities or souls in the beginning. For, the beginnings of sin, of course, were in seeking expression of themselves outside of the plan or the way in which God had expressed same. Thus it was the individual, see?

Having given free will, then—though having the foreknowledge, though being omnipotent and omnipresent—it is only when the soul that is a portion of God *chooses* that God knows the end thereof.

⁶(Q) The fourth problem concerns man's tenancy on earth. Was it originally intended that souls remain out of earthly forms, and were the races originated as a necessity resulting from error?

(A) The earth and its manifestations were only the expression of God and not necessarily as a place of tenancy for the souls of men, until man was created—to meet the needs of existing conditions.

⁷(Q) The fifth problem concerns an explanation of the life readings. From a study of these it seems that there is a trend downward, from early incarnations, toward greater earthliness and less mentality. Then there is a swing upward, accompanied by suffering, patience, and understanding. Is this the normal pattern, which results in virtue and oneness with God obtained by free will and mind?

(A) This is correct. It is the pattern as it is set in Him.

⁸(Q) The sixth problem concerns interplanetary and inter-system dwelling, between earthly lives. It was given through this source that the entity Edgar Cayce, after the experience as Uhjltd, went to the system of Arcturus, and then returned to earth. Does this indicate a usual or an unusual step in soul evolution?

(A) As indicated, or as has been indicated in other sources besides this as respecting this very problem— Arcturus is that which may be called the center of this universe, through which individuals pass and at which period there comes the choice of the individual as to whether it is to return to complete there—that is, in this planetary system, our sun, the earth sun and its planetary system—or to pass on to others. This was an unusual step, and yet a usual one.

[9](Q) The seventh problem concerns implications from the sixth problem. Is it necessary to finish the solar system cycle before going to other systems?

(A) Necessary to finish the solar cycle.

[10](Q) Can oneness be attained—or the finish of evolution reached—on any system, or must it be in a particular one?

(A) Depending upon what system the entity has entered, to be sure. It may be completed in any of the many systems.

[11](Q) Must the solar cycle be finished on earth, or can it be completed on another planet, or does each planet have a cycle of its own which must be finished?

(A) If it is begun on the earth it must be finished on the earth. The solar system of which the earth is a part is only a portion of the whole. For, as indicated in the number of planets about the earth, they are of one and the same—and they are relative one to another. It is the cycle of the whole system that is finished, see?

[12](Q) The eighth problem concerns the pattern made by parents at conception. Should it be said that this pattern attracts a certain soul because it approximates conditions which that soul wishes to work with?

(A) It approximates conditions. It does not set. For, the individual entity or soul, given the opportunity, has its own free will to work in or out of those problems as presented by that very union. Yet the very union, of course, attracts or brings a channel or an opportunity for the expression of an individual entity.

[13](Q) Does the incoming soul take on of necessity some of the parents' karma?

(A) Because of its relative relationship to same, yes. Otherwise, no.

[14](Q) Does the soul itself have an earthly pattern which fits back into the one created by the parents?

(A) Just as indicated, it is relative—as one related to another; and because of the union of activities they are brought in the pattern. For in such there is the explanation of universal or divine laws, which are ever one and the same; as indicated in the expression that God moved within Himself and then He didn't change, though did bring to Himself that of His own being made crucified even in the flesh.

[15](Q) Are there several patterns which a soul might take on, depending on what phase of development it wished to work upon—i.e., could a soul choose to be one of several personalities, any of which would fit its individuality?

(A) Correct.

[16](Q) Is the average fulfillment of the soul's expectation more or less than fifty percent?

(A) It's a continuous advancement, so it is more than fifty percent.

[17](Q) Are hereditary, environment, and will equal factors in aiding or retarding the entity's development?

(A) Will is the greater factor, for it may overcome any or all of the others; provided that will is made one with the pattern, see? For, no influence of heredity, environment or whatnot, surpasses the will; else why would there have been that pattern shown in which the individual soul, no matter how far astray it may have gone, may enter with Him into the holy of holies?

[18](Q) The ninth problem concerns the proper symbols, or similes, for the Master, the Christ. Should Jesus be described as the soul who first went through the cycle of earthly lives to attain perfection, including perfection in the planetary lives also?

(A) He should be. This is as the man, see?

[19](Q) Should this be described as a voluntary mission One Who was already perfected and returned to God, having accomplished His Oneness in other planes and systems?

(A) Correct.

[20](Q) Should the Christ Consciousness be described as the awareness within each soul, imprinted in pattern on the mind and waiting to be awakened by the will, of the soul's oneness with God?

(A) Correct. That's the idea exactly!

[21](Q) Please list the names of the incarnations of the Christ, and of Jesus, indicating where the development of the man Jesus began.

(A) First, in the beginning, of course; and then as Enoch, Melchizedek, in the perfection. Then in the earth of Joseph, Joshua, Jeshua, Jesus.

[22](Q) The tenth problem concerns the factors of soul evolution. Should mind, the builder, be described as the last development because it should not unfold until it has a firm foundation of emotional virtues?

(A) This might be answered Yes and No, both. But if it is presented in that there is kept, willfully, see, that desire to be in the at-onement, then it is necessary for that attainment before it recognizes mind as the way.

[23](Q) The eleventh problem concerns a parallel with Christianity. Is Gnosticism the closest type of Christianity to that which is given through this source?

(A) This is a parallel, and was the commonly accepted one until there began to be set rules in which there were the attempts to take shortcuts. And there are none in Christianity!

[24](Q) What action of the early church, or council, can be mentioned as that which ruled reincarnation from Christian theology?

(A) Just as indicated—the attempts of individuals to

accept or take advantage of, because of this knowledge, see?

[25](Q) Do souls become entangled in other systems as they did in this system?

(A) In other systems that represent the same as the earth does in this system, yes.

[26](Q) Is there any other advice which may be given to this entity at this time in the preparation of these chapters?

(A) Hold fast to that ideal, and using Him ever as the Ideal. And hold up that *necessity* for each to meet the same problems. And *do not* attempt to shed or to surpass or go around the Cross. *This* is that upon which each and every soul *must* look and know it is to be borne in self *with* Him.

[27]We are through for the present.

Chapter 2

THE LAWS OF LIVING

READING 1567-2

The Cayce readings—like all outstanding philosophies—present the universe as a lawful, orderly place. Events occur with rhyme and reason. Human development unfolds with dependable rules. In reading 1567-2, Cayce spells out the essential principles of his philosophy in perhaps its most succinct and direct expression.

In many ways this reading represents Cayce the metaphysician at his best. Metaphysics is a time-honored branch of philosophy that deals largely with two issues:

- The nature of existence and being (ontology), and
- The orderly systems of the universe (cosmology).

Cayce deals eloquently with both in this reading. He speaks of who we really are and how we came into being. He addresses the question of God's most basic nature. In addition, he speaks of the laws that govern our experience—for example, the deeper meaning of astrology, and the roles of mind and will in shaping our experiences. These four points stand out as centerpieces of Cayce's metaphysical system:

- All life is an expression of the one God, who truly exists. God is not a figment of human imagination—not something that people dreamed up because they feared death. God is the foundation of all that is. Furthermore, the life that comes from God is continuous, and therefore our own lives as spiritual beings go on beyond the grave.

• Life is purposeful. God started with a plan for us as souls; and, even though each of us chose to drift away (i.e., made an "error in individual activity"), that plan is still available. The good news about the plan is that it's all-inclusive—not only having room for everyone but also having room for all aspects of ourselves: spiritually, mentally, and physically. That means that to discover and fulfill God's plan won't require a denial of any phase of human experience.

• The outer universe is represented in our own inner makeup. The microcosm reflects the macrocosm—and vice versa. Things that happen on a grand scale in the universe also happen within us on a personal scale. One illustration of this principle is found in astrology. Cayce supports the fundamental premise of astrology: the planets and the stars have a relationship to human temperament and behavior. But he differs from many astrologers in the area of causation. The fact that Mars was on the ascendant at the moment of one person's birth doesn't force her to be a certain way as an adult. In Cayce's metaphysical system, it's almost the other way around. Because of experience that soul had before birth (in so-called interplanetary sojourns), it chose to be born at a moment when the planets would depict (i.e., "bear witness to") its own innate patterns.

• Each of us has the power of creation and the freedom of will. Mind and will are the two attributes with which each soul can use spiritual energy. Mind exists with a foot in each of two worlds. One aspect is focused on material life; another, on the spiritual world. In both of its aspects, mind has the potential to be creative. But it's the will that determines what the mind will build.

It's the will—the "ability to choose for self"—that favors one influence over another. And in so doing, the will shapes the very essence of one's character and individuality.

As valuable as these four principles are, nevertheless, we need to look for an even broader message in reading 1567-2. Cayce is more than *a teacher of metaphysics,* and this reading clearly shows that added dimension. His philosophy goes beyond how and why things are the way they are. He adds the dimension of ethics, moral values, and purposes. It's that extra ingredient that gives the Cayce philosophy its depth and spirituality.

We miss the point of Cayce's life and work if we reduce him to metaphysics exclusively. Admittedly, it's sometimes easy to underplay instances where Cayce goes beyond the role of metaphysician. And why do we miss it? Our oversight is probably because he does such a good job answering tough metaphysical questions. For example, reading 1567-2 is full of fascinating clues and nuggets of wisdom about many riddles of our existence. But in our delight at finding such a treasure chest of explanations, will we also notice the other vital dimension to the Cayce philosophy? Will we see that scattered among the profound statements about an orderly universe there are other secrets being revealed?

Let's look carefully at this reading and notice also some of these quieter, less sensational truths. They don't address abstract questions about the nature of being or the orderly systems of the universe. Instead they are statements about ideals and purposes. They are teachings that are ethical and values-driven. Two stand out in this reading.

• There is meaning in suffering. It's not simply punishment for things we've done wrong in the past. It's probably unavoidable that each of us will experience disappointment, frustration, separation, and pain. As the Buddha indicates, that's just the character of physical life. Or as Cayce states, we've entered into a realm of "trials of body and of mind" that tend to cloud the glories we might see. But the important news is that even suffering can serve a higher purpose. It's especially at those points where we're being tested that we may be open to receive the reassuring, healing grace of the Divine.

What does this spiritual principle teach us about values and ideals? Simply a new way of seeing our own points of pain and vulnerability. Shame and guilt aren't appropriate. The points in life where we're hurting have something to teach us—they are the spots at which quiet encounters with the Spirit may be most likely to come.

• We are responsible to each other. The whole ball game rests with how we treat our fellow human beings. We aren't so much responsible for each other, but we do have vital obligations to one another. In fact, it's in the social realm that we have the best chance to succeed in the purpose for which any soul comes into materiality. We're here to become aware of our relationship to God, and that happens primarily by what we think, say, and do with other human beings.

Taken together, these two facets of Cayce's thought give us the big picture of his overall philosophy—the insightful metaphysical laws that teach us why things are the way they are, alongside the quieter, more modest reminders of what we need to value most of all. When we notice, understand, and then apply what the Cayce readings have to offer from *both* streams of wisdom, then we've become students of this material in the deepest sense.

THE READING

This psychic reading, 1567-2, was given by Edgar Cayce on May 26, 1938. The conductor was Gertrude Cayce.

[1]EC: Yes, we have the records here of that entity now known as or called Miss [1567].

[2]These as we find may be said to be very beautiful records, yet in ways such that it may be questioned by some as to why one who has been so far advanced in some experiences has been so little in the limelight or in the position of prominence through the same ways in the present.

[3]If the varied experiences are studied with an eye single to service, these may possibly be understood or comprehended. For remember that God looketh on the heart and not, as man, upon the outward appearances.

[4]Hence there are lessons to be gained by the entity from even those feelings, those innate urges that cry for expression. For in their very expression, not finding outlet they turn as it were upon those influences from within.

[5]But we find that if these are used, the entity may yet find a peace, a manner or way of expression that will bring joy into the experience in this sojourn.

[6]In giving the interpretations, know that these are chosen with the purpose that they are to become helpful experiences.

[7]An experience, then, is not only a happening, but what is the reaction in your own mind? What does it do to you to make your life, your habits, your relationships to others of a more helpful nature, with a more hopeful attitude?

[8]These are the criterions for every individual's experience—sincerity of purpose, of desire; putting the whole law into effect in the activities—which is to love the Lord

thy God with all thy heart, thy mind, thy body, and thy neighbor as thyself.

⁹This is the whole law. All the other things given or written are only the interpreting of same.

¹⁰Then what does such a proclaiming preclude? From what basis is the reasoning drawn? What is the purpose of an individual experience of an entity or soul into the earth at any given period?

¹¹These answered then give a background for the interpreting of *why.*

¹²There are urges latent and manifested in the experience of each soul, each entity, each body.

¹³First we begin with the fact that God *is;* and that the heavens and the earth, and all nature, declare this. Just as there is the longing within *every* heart for the continuity of life.

¹⁴What then is life? As it has been given, in Him we live and move and have our being. Then He, God, *is!* Or life in all of its phases, its expressions, is a manifestation of that force or power we call God, or that is called God.

¹⁵Then life is continuous. For that force, that power which has brought the earth, the universe and all the influences in same into being, is a continuous thing—is a first premise.

¹⁶All glory, all honor then, is *due* that creative force that may be manifested in our experiences as individuals through the manner in which we deal with our fellow man!

¹⁷Then we say, when our loved ones, our heart's desires are taken from us, in what are we to believe?

¹⁸This we find is only answered in that which has been given as His promise, that God hath not willed that any soul should perish but hath with every temptation, every trial, every disappointment made a way of escape or for correcting same. It is not a way of justification only, as by faith, but a way to know, to realize that in these dis-

appointments, separations, there comes the assurance that He cares!

[19]For to be absent from the body is to be present with that consciousness that we, as an individual, have worshiped as our God! For as we do it unto the least of our brethren, our associates, our acquaintance, our servants day by day, so we do unto our Maker!

[20]What is the purpose then, we ask, for our entering into this vale, or experience, or awareness, where disappointments, fears, trials of body and of mind appear to mount above all of the glories that we may see?

[21]In the beginning, when there was the creating, or the calling of individual entities into being, we were made to be the companions with the Father-God.

[22]Now flesh and blood may not inherit eternal life; only the spirit, only the purpose, only the desire may inherit same.

[23]Then that error in individual activity—not of another but of ourselves, individually—separated us from that awareness.

[24]Hence God prepared the way through flesh whereby all phases of spirit, mind and body might express.

[25]The earth then is a three-dimensional, a three-phase or three-manner expression. Just as the Father, the Son, the Holy Spirit are one. So are our body, mind and soul one—in Him.

[26]Now we have seen, we have heard, we know that the Son represents or signifies the Mind.

[27]He, the Son, was in the earth-earthy even as we—and yet is of the Godhead.

[28]Hence the Mind is both material and spiritual, and taketh hold on that which is its environ, its want, in our experiences.

[29]Then Mind, as He, was the Word—and dwelt among men; and we beheld Him as the face of the Father.

[30]So is our mind made, so does our mind conceive—

even as He; and *is* the builder.

[31]Then that our mind dwells upon, that our mind feeds upon, that do we supply to our body—yes, to our soul!

[32]Hence we find all of these are the background, as it were, for the interpreting of our experience, of our sojourns in the earth.

[33]For the astrological or the relative position of the earth (our immediate home) is not the center of the universe, is not the center of our thought; but the kingdom of the Father or the kingdom of Heaven is within! Why? Because our mind, the Son, is within us.

[34]Then with that consciousness of His awareness, we may know even as He has given, "Ye abide in me, as I in the Father— I will come and abide with thee."

[35]In that consciousness, then, the purposes for which each soul enters materiality are that it may become aware of its relationships to the Creative Forces or God; by the material manifestation of the things thought, said, *done,* in relation to its fellow man!

[36]As the earth then occupies its three-dimensional phase of experience in our own solar system, and as each of those companions that are about the solar system represents as it were one of the phases of our conscience— the elements of our understanding—or our senses; then they each in their place, in their plane, bear a relationship to us, even as our desires for physical sustenance; that is: foods for the body; with all of the attributes, all of the abilities to take that we feed upon and turn it into elements for our body.

[37]All of the elements are gathered from that upon which we have fed to build blood, bone, hair, nails; the sight, the hearing, the touching, the feelings, the expressions.

[38]Why? Because these are *quickened* by the presence of the spirit of the Creative Force (within).

[39]So our mind, with its attributes, gathers from that upon which we feed in our mental self; forming our con-

cepts of our relationship with those things that are con-
trariwise to His biddings or in line with that law which is
all-inclusive; that is, the love of the Father, with our
mind, our body, our soul, and our neighbor as self.

⁴⁰Then all of these influences astrological (as known
or called) from without, bear witness—or *are* as innate
influences upon our activity, our sojourn through any
given experience. Not because we were born with the
sun in this sign or that, nor because Jupiter or Mercury
or Saturn or Uranus or Mars was rising or setting, but
rather:

⁴¹Because we were made for the purpose of being
companions with Him, a little lower than the angels who
behold His face ever yet as heirs, as joint heirs with Him
who *is* the Savior, the Way, then we have brought these
about *because* of our activities through our *experiences* in
those realms! Hence they bear witness by being *in* certain positions—because of our activity, our sojourn in
those environs, in relationships to the universal forces
of activity.

⁴²Hence they bear witness of certain urges in us, not
beyond our will but controlled by our will!

⁴³For as was given of old, there is each day set before
us life and death, good and evil. We choose because of
our natures. If our will were broken, if we were com-
manded to do this or that, or to become as an automa-
ton, our individuality then would be lost and we would
only be as in Him without conscience—*conscience*—
(consciousness) of being one with Him; with the abilities to choose for self!

⁴⁴For we *can,* as God say yea to this, nay to that; we
can order this or the other in our experience, by the very
gifts that have been given or appointed unto our keeping. For we are indeed as laborers, co-laborers in the
vineyard of the Lord—or of they that are fearful of His
coming.

⁴⁵And we choose each day *whom* we will serve! And by the records in time and space, as we have moved through the realms of His kingdom, we have left our mark upon same.

⁴⁶Then they influence us, either directly or indirectly, in the manner as we have declared ourselves in favor of this or that influence in our material experience. And by the casting of our lot in this or that direction, we bring into our experience the influence in that manner.

⁴⁷For this entity, then, we find these as influences:

⁴⁸Venus—the beauty ye enjoy; the abilities that are a part of thy whole experience. The abilities of love, yet that have in a manner been denied thee when ye consider as to thy material surroundings, thy material undertakings; but in thy deeper self ye find these as a part of thy experience—apparently as yet never satisfied, or that thou hast loved, that thou hast taken to thy heart has been swept away from thee, taken to those influences or environs that to thee become as naught!

⁴⁹Then there must be through these very influences and channels an outlet, a manner in which these may find expression; which there is, in thy ability to *write beautiful* things that will act and react upon the minds and the hearts of others—those that may read, those that may make same to be a part of their experience by the very manner in which ye in loving care may show forth these in thy dealings with thy fellow man!

⁵⁰In Jupiter we find the benevolent influences. And as there is the conjunction of Venus and Jupiter, which will appear in the coming fall—or about October the 13th should be one of or *the* most glorious days, as a day, for thy experiences of wondrous things that may be an answer to thy longings in many directions; the knowledge of those very things that may bring the awareness, the consciousness of His abiding presence that is nigh unto thee ever!

[51]In these ye may be favored with the greater comprehension.

[52]As to thy experiences or appearances in the earth, thy sojourns among men—these have been, as indicated, beautiful in many manners, in many ways; and yet they seem so for naught in the present!

[53]But drawing nigh unto the Father-God (within) ye may become more and more aware of thy purposes for being here. For His promise is to bring to thy remembrance all those things from the foundations of the earth!

[54]Hence from the very activities these find expression in the present in thy love for history, historical subjects, things pertaining to influences brought because of the relationships of individuals to conditions and characters and places! These become in thy activities and in thy abilities but channels, means through which ye may bring some of that beauty, some of that joy that is in His promises to thee, and to thy fellow man in thy very activity!

[55]Before this, then, we find the entity was in the land of the present nativity during those periods prior to and during what is known as the American Revolution.

[56]For the entity then was among those peoples about that fort then called Dearborn, who overran the land or who prepared for the indwellings and homes for others in the land.

[57]When the associates and companions of the entity then, as Mae Marandal, escaped and established dwellings in the hills (where there later became great orchards, above the hills of thy own present abode), the entity brought much to those peoples in the manner and the way of keeping the records. The entity brought much through the giving of the greater understanding as to how there might be the rotation of this or that in the activity to bring about conveniences in the experiences of the people.

58And ye loved thy neighbors; they loved thee!

59For oft many, many came to thee for counsel, for that thou had been able to give to thine own, to thine own household, to thy own neighborhood, to thy own surroundings!

60And in the present, in the application of those abilities arising from that sojourn, ye may find the abilities to give to others; not to shut thyself in, either in body or mind, but *open* thy heart, *open* thy abilities to others!

61Write—write—write! Though ye may tear up for a year, or for more than a year everything ye write giving expression to same, ye will find the abilities to bring into the experience and minds of others the joys that are not even comprehended in the present!

62Before that we find the entity was in the Persian and Arabian land, during those periods when in the "city in the hills and the plains" that teacher Uhjltd made overtures to the experiences of men to put away their petty feelings, their petty hates, those things that made people afraid by the very power of might making right; realizing that the power of love makes right.

63The entity was among the natives who were of the household of that Uhjltd, and an older—much older sister of the entity in the experience, in the name then Ujdelda.

64With the establishing of the activities and the household being gathered about the entity, we find that this entity made for helpful activities with that teacher Uhjltd; and stood with the peoples against the rebellions that arose among a portion of the nomads during the early part of the activity.

65Again during those periods when the Greeks and a portion of the peoples from the Persian land brought turmoils, the entity then aided in keeping that equilibrium—by what? The accounts of what had been the prices paid as it were by individuals, by those who had been cleansed in body and mind; not materially but mentally, spiritually!

⁶⁶Thus the beauty of such unfoldments made for experiences that brought joy and happiness to the entity in that sojourn—as it may in the applying of self in those directions associated with the activities in that experience; in spreading the gospel as it were of good tidings, by that same teacher; in being a portion of that group to aid in the publications of facts—not only of those things that may be gathered by self but that have been a part of the gatherings of others.

⁶⁷Before that we find the entity was in the Egyptian land, now called, when there were those activities being disseminated through the varied lands for which preparations had been made for or by individuals that might bring into the experience of material activity the greater means or manners of expression.

⁶⁸The entity then was among those who were in the activities of the Temple Beautiful, that made for the preparations of the many.

⁶⁹Thus the entity, as She-Lula-Or-Ar, made for the channels through which there arose the teachers who became especially fitted for activities or operations overseas, or the beginning of those that became the greater active upon the waves of the oceans and seas.

⁷⁰As to the abilities of the entity in the present, then:

⁷¹Hold fast to that which is latent and may be so manifested in that love ye hold for those of princely, crowning glories in the experiences ye have enjoyed in the earth!

⁷²Study to show thyself approved unto God, a workman not ashamed; rightly divining—dividing—the words of truth, keeping thy own self in thy own good conscience unspotted from questionings within thy own self.

⁷³Write—*write*—of Him; of those experiences of thy own!

[74]And join thyself with those things being undertaken by thy brother-teacher of old!

[75]Thus ye shall know peace and happiness *here—now!*

[76]We are through for the present.

Chapter 3

PATIENCE

READING 262-25

Patience may well be the most mysterious virtue described in the Cayce readings. In part this is because Cayce ascribes such importance to it. Patience is called one of the essential dimensions of material life. Along with time and space, patience is a fundamental measurement of a soul's experience in the physical world. Many students of the readings have puzzled over just this idea. What does it mean to say that the three-dimensional world is created by time, space, and patience? The first two ingredients make more immediate sense than the last.

Reading 262-25 can help us see what Cayce meant by patience. It's one of three given to the original "A Search for God" group as they gathered material in order to write the seventh lesson in this spiritual growth sequence. Made up largely of personal messages to individual group members, we see a mosaic in which Cayce's overall philosophy about patience begins to emerge. Simply because these people were living very ordinary lives, the patience-demanding challenges they faced were exactly like what most of us face today.

Several fundamental qualities about patience are

prominent in this mosaic. First is how closely patience is linked to one's spiritual ideal. Through patience one achieves an active relationship with that ideal. Patience isn't sitting around waiting. It's not feeling satisfied with the status quo. Instead, patience gets us into the thick of life and allows us to implement whatever spiritual ideal we've chosen. How is this done? By our reactions to the challenging opportunities which arise. Patience is the dimension which measures our responses to the unavoidable problems, difficulties, and hardships of living. It's in those responses that we have the chance to demonstrate the ideal we've chosen.

Second, patience is a consciousness-expander. In the short discourse of 262-25 which precedes the questions and answers, this quality is featured. Through patience we become more aware of how our souls are growing and developing. Patience is called "that necessary activity of the mind . . . that makes for expansion . . . "

One way to interpret this expansion is in terms of our understanding of life's purposefulness. Events don't occur randomly or arbitrarily. Life is meaningful and every challenge has purpose behind it. Patience creates an expansion of consciousness and allows us to see with new eyes. This angle on patience is reminiscent of teachings presented by longtime student of the Cayce material, the late J. Everett Irion. In elaborating on Cayce's novel concept of patience as the third dimension, Irion defined it as "understanding the purposefulness of a manifest idea." That is to say, when an idea (defined by Cayce as the fourth dimension, where "mind is the builder") manifests into the three-dimensional, physical world, we're challenged to comprehend its meaning and purpose. Through patience that understanding is possible.

A third quality of patience emphasized in 262-25 is focus on the here-and-now. Notice how often in this reading there can be found reminders about the present moment. It's worded in different ways but always with a nudge to come back to the present moment:

"Today, now, is the accepted time!"

" . . . look not back; remember Lot's wife."

"Let each live, then, as though they *expected* their concept of the Master Christ to *dine* with them today."

Cayce was never one to advise forgetting the past or ignoring the prudent demands to plan for the future. But his emphasis on patience—which is so evident from his naming it as the third dimension itself—makes it clear where most of our attention should be: in the present moment, here-and-now, today. We get ourselves in trouble when we don't pay enough attention to what's going on around us and inside of us right now.

Often, that's very hard to do. We live in a culture that features nostalgic, sentimental tugs to the past, *and* impatient, desire-inducing propaganda about what we ought to have in our future. Where are the forces that bring our attention back to the here-and-now, so that we can mine the rich treasures of the present moment? *Those forces must come from within ourselves.* That is patience.

Imagine a situation in which you have the chance to experience patience. It will be some type of difficulty—perhaps an illness, a financial problem, or even just an obstacle to the day progressing the way you planned it. How can patience work to expand your awareness so that you discover the purposefulness in that situation? The key will be to move your attention as fully as possible into the present moment. Take in the sights, sounds, and conditions. Pay attention to what's going on—not what you wish was happening instead. "Use that at hand," as this reading puts it. See where and how this is a chance for you to express your ideals in some specific way. In that simple, meditative-like exercise with your mind and will, you've fully made use of the third dimension: patience.

THE READING

This psychic reading, 262-25, was given by Edgar Cayce on August 7, 1932. The conductor was Gertrude Cayce.

[1]GC: You will have before you members of the study group present in this room, and their work on the lesson of *patience,* an outline of which I hold in my hand. You will please give us that information which we will need in expanding this outline, and suggest any changes or additions that would be advisable in the approach to this subject. You will answer questions which various members will ask.

[2]EC: Yes, we have the group as gathered here, as a group and as individuals. Also the work on preparing the lessons—the lesson in patience.

[3]As is seen in this outline, this is very good. The expansions should be rather in this direction, that the activity of patience is meekness in action, pureness in heart, that makes for those forces enabling one to become aware and conscious of their soul's expansion with the creative energies in the activities of the spiritual life. As there is the expansion of the spiritual forces of the material body, the reflections from same are those attributes that make for the expressing of the Christ life in the daily walks of the body. So that love in its essence is manifested in every word, act, thought and experience of the body, even as it was in Him. Patience is that necessary activity of the mind, mentally, physically, spiritually, that makes for expansion of and acquaintance with the activities of that that may be known in self, as to whether there *is* the proper attitude with that which is held as the ideal, as to whether the faith is in faith or by works, whether the virtue is as with understanding or is as a set rule, whether self is in possession of the ideal, and with cooperative measures activating in the experience of individuals.

Hence, as we find, this lesson must be the summing up of all that has been experienced by individuals through that they have given to others, that they now must live themselves in their daily activities—that they may enter in. Ready for questions.

[4](Q) [307]: How may I more perfectly live the life, that I may through patience gain the understanding?

(A) In the application of that known day by day. The Spirit does not call on anyone to live that it does not already know and understand. In the doing does there come the knowledge, the understanding for the next step. Today, now, is the accepted time! Those that will enter in will trust in that they have through faith and with patience wait for that necessary activity for the next step. Use that in hand.

[5](Q) [303]: Is there a message for me that will help me in the practice of more perfect patience?

(A) As the trust, the hope, the faith is manifested by the patience day by day does there become the more awareness in self's own inner consciousness that all is well with Him; knowing that if the Lord is on thy side, who may be against you? Trust, and do that thou knowest to do, acting as the spirit moves within—and look not back; remember Lot's wife.

[6](Q) [560]: In reading of July 24, 1932, [262-24] what was meant by "Be mad but sin not"? Please explain.

(A) One that may control self in anger is beginning the first lessons or laws of experience. One that may control self in anger, that must come as resentment in the speech of individuals, may make for that which disregards the words said; disliking that which would produce such a feeling within self, yet able to love the soul of one that causes or produces such a state of feeling. This is patience, and love, and hope, and meekness, and pureness of heart. The meek shall inherit the earth, said He—the pure in heart shall see God. They are promises!

Believest thou Him? Then be angry and sin not is to know that these are thine *own* promises—to thee—to thee!

⁷(Q) In patience am I expressing "Possess ye your soul"? If not, please simplify how I may do so.

(A) All make that expression in whatever their activity may be; for that is as a truth that one becomes conscious of, aware of, that possession that makes them one with, a child of, the living God; for flesh and blood does not inherit the possessions with Him, but the spirit makes alive that soul that is aware of His consciousness in a material, a mental, or a spiritual plane. Hence all express this in whatever their actions be. As to whether this or that individual is doing this in the manner another would do so, this is to judge. Who is the judge? He that giveth judgment! The individual's soul, that would be one with Him.

⁸(Q) [413]: What has really happened to an individual when they think their patience has completely worn out?

(A) They have lost patience with themselves.

⁹(Q) [379]: Is there any message for me that will help me to more perfectly practice patience in all my work and under all conditions?

(A) Be faithful to that which is given in thy charge day by day, for he that is faithful over the little things will be made the ruler over the many. Those who have gained that consciousness of the indwelling of that Spirit, that is abiding with those who seek to know His face, have the consciousness that this *is* the day, the time, when all men must seek to be patient one with another, under all conditions and circumstances, that they may be one with Him who in patience endured all that we might have the access to the Father, through the patience, the love, the consciousness, shown in a material plane. Be faithful to that thou *knowest* to do. Question not what nor whether another has chosen. Rather do that *thou* knowest to do.

[10](Q) What time is referred to in James 5:8, "Be ye patient; establish your hearts, for the coming of the Lord draweth nigh"?

(A) As just given, this is the time—today—when the time draweth nigh for each soul to become more aware of the necessity of magnifying *His* presence through the patience borne one to, one with, one of another, that He may be glorified in us, through the promise of the Father that such will be to those that love His coming. Let each live, then, as though they *expected* their concept of the Master Christ to *dine* with them today. What *would* ye have to offer as the fruits of thine own life, thine thoughts, thine acts, thine deeds? For, "Inasmuch as ye have done it unto the least of these my little ones ye have done it unto me."

[11](Q) [585]: Is it the lack of patience that causes me to find my problems so hard to overcome? If so, how may I gain the necessary patience to overcome these problems?

(A) As has been given, first—Is thine ideal only in Him? Is thine self in accord with thine ideal? Is thine virtue and understanding in accord with these? Then with patience wait for that awakening which will make for an understanding of that necessary to overcome—even as He. Taking stock, then, with self, one may know whether it is patience, faith, virtue, knowledge, brotherly love, or what, lacking in self. Do not find the fault in the other, but rather cleanse thine *own* mind, heart, and soul; and the proper attitude toward whatever problem that presents itself will be in that manner of understanding love that knows no fear, but being content in *His* praise, His love, His understanding.

[12](Q) From time to time I have had to come into my room a friend who has passed on. Is this contact harmful or beneficial?

(A) In this, there are always those seeking that we may

help, that may help us; for as we help another does help come to us. Pray for that friend, that the way through the shadows may be easier for them. It becomes easier for you.

[13](Q) [993]: Is there a message for me that will help me to practice patience?

(A) Use that thou knowest, and with patience wait for the light that comes with the knowledge of "I am using that Thou gavest me."

[14](Q) [69]: When one has gotten the understanding of the oneness with the Father-Mother-God, why is it one does not experience the joy and bliss, and overcome all inharmony, which is their divine birthright? May I have the answer from Master Jesus, if possible?

(A) Then, with patience wait for that. Is that attained in thine self so that the Consciousness of the Master comes to thee in all thine hours, then with patience wait ye on the Lord; for as one finds that in the understanding of the Oneness, when *He* has *found* that the vessel is worthy of acceptation it is *kept* full.

[15](Q) [2125]: You told me [in 262-24] that anyone could do automatic writing. Will you please tell me how I may develop it?

(A) By practice. Sit alone with pencil and paper, and let that guide that may be sought—or may come in—direct. It will come. Anyone may; but is it the better may oft be the question? This may only be the better when surrounding self with those influences that may bring those of the *constructive* forces alone.

[16](Q) Who is giving me this message?

(A) That one sought from.

[17](Q) Compilers: Is there any message to the compilers?

(A) Take that given, in how the expansion should be, and weave it into that which has been given in, in such a manner that it may become a blessing to those who seek.

[18]We are through for the present.

Chapter 4

THE MISSION OF THE SOUL

READING 442-3

How am I doing? That's a question we may often wonder to ourselves. Am I making it? Am I doing what I'm here to do?

The man who received this reading had the benefit of Edgar Cayce's psychic counsel to help answer the question. Twice before he had gotten assistance from Mr. Cayce. Now he was asking for a penetrating assessment of his inner and outer development—a sort of spiritual audit.

What he received on this occasion was a profound description of the spiritual tasks that we *all* face. He was given a picture of the human soul and its essential job while in the earth dimension.

First is the principle that soul development requires an ideal—spiritual growth happens in the context of having chosen a purpose or direction. It's not something that simply happens to us, like losing baby teeth when we start grade school or finding that our hair is turning gray in mid-life. Soul development necessitates choices and initiative on our part.

More specifically, Cayce recommends certain ideals: patience and tolerance. What is it about these qualities that contributes so significantly to the mission of the soul? Both of them force us to shift gears and to look at life in a new way. Patience and tolerance require us to *go beyond the appearance of things.* In other words, these two qualities require a shift in consciousness so that we see and feel events in a different way.

When we're patient, we have a new sense of time; when we're tolerant, we see the behaviors of other people in a way that leaves room for understanding and forgiveness. Neither quality makes much sense from a materialistic point of view. The appearance of things says that we're going to miss the boat if we don't hurry up, or that people are going to get the best of us if we let them be offensive. But even though patience and tolerance don't always seem very logical, they awaken us to realize that we are souls. That very awareness is a key part of our mission in the earth dimension.

But what exactly is the soul? When that awakening begins, what is it that we realize about ourselves? Two features in particular: immortality and individuality. As this reading puts it, we start to sense "the continuity of life . . . [that] which lives on and on . . . " And furthermore, we awaken to our own uniqueness and freedom— "that which is individual of each and every body as it finds expression in the material world . . . "

Of course, this is all much easier said than done. It's no small task in the modern world to be patient and tolerant, even occasionally. But on this very point Cayce offers a promise: If we don't succumb to the fatigue of loving service—if we don't become "weary in well-doing"—then we're given the crown of life. This lovely metaphor refers to a distinct state of consciousness that comes like a gift as we sincerely try to live the mission of the soul. In essence Cayce defines this gift as *the ability to know that one is in accord with divine protection.* That is to say, we're not cut loose and adrift in the material

world. The Spirit is with us—protecting us—as we pa-
tiently and tolerantly work on the mission of the soul.
What's the basic character of that mission? In the most
fundamental terms, what are we supposed to do while
we're here? Is it to pay off bad karma from past lives?
That's the possibility Mr. [442] poses in his question
about "karmic debts from previous life experiences." But
on that point Cayce admits there are challenges that are
rooted in the past, and they must be met. But he goes on
to remind us that there is a higher way to transform
those errors and wounds, a way that depends on seeing
the real character of the soul's mission.

The basic character of our task is simple—that is, the
job is straightforward and uncomplicated, though surely
not easy. Any soul's mission in the earth plane is to (1)
apply and live out *what you know,* and (2) meet creatively with all your resources *what comes to you.* This
second point is found again and again in this particular
reading. It's a theme—a refrain—in Cayce's message
about our mission. For example:

• " . . . doing with a might in the Lord that thy hands
find to do."

• "Tend His lambs, those that are in thy way, those
thou meetest day by day."

• "That that is given thee put to use . . . "

These sorts of statements are powerful reminders that
we don't have to go out looking for great challenges to
prove ourselves. Success with the soul's mission doesn't
require any restless search for spiritual opportunity. Life
itself presents the occasions.

Something in us may not be satisfied at first with answers like this. "The Mission of the Soul" somehow
sounds more grand—it suggests great deeds of cosmic
proportion, not something as mundane as patient tolerance with the difficulties that pop up each day. In fact,
the Cayce readings themselves are sometimes criticized

for not being sophisticated enough, for leaving out eso-
teric details and relying too often on spiritual basics. But
are we ready for the details if we can't yet deal with the
fundamentals? No doubt there are also more complex
ways of articulating the mission of the soul and the steps
of spiritual evolution. (In other readings many of those
details are described.) But this reading is actually doing
us a favor. It strips away the metaphysical sidelights and
stays focused on what will truly determine if this lifetime
is to be spiritually successful.

THE READING

*This psychic reading, 442-3, was given by Edgar Cayce
on January 26, 1934. The conductor was Hugh Lynn
Cayce.*

(HLC: You will give a mental and spiritual reading for
him, giving the reason for entrance into this cycle of experience and detailed guidance for the development and
expression of his inner soul faculties in this present life.)

[1]EC: Yes, we have the entity here, [442].

[2]In considering the activities of the mental and soul
body of an entity, in relations to its activities or its purposes in any given experience, something of that which
has been built in the soul development is necessary
to be referred to as comparison, that there may be presented in a comprehensible way and manner that for
mental and soul expansion in any given activity.

[3]In this entity, [442], we find in the varied experiences
or appearances through its activity in the environs, more
of the developments than of retardments. While in varied experiences there are seen periods when indecisions
and the particular activity made for rather the retarding,
in the whole we have found that with the application of
that which has become apparent in the present experi-

ence—as to what has been set as the ideals and principles by which the application of life in a given appearance or experience may be in a direction or in
accordance with the entity's own judgments—the development has been in accord with an ideal. Making for,
then, in self, patience—which has been pointed by Him
who is the Giver of life as being the qualification in every
entity's experience through the application of which every entity becomes aware of possessing a soul, that
birthright which is the gift of the Father to each and every entity that may be presented before the Throne of
Thrones, before the Holy of Holies, in a holy and acceptable way and manner.

⁴In righteousness, then—as is found in patience, that
has become the worthy attribute of the soul of this entity, in tolerance and in patience, has come the awareness of the continuity of life—and that the soul is that
which is individual of each and every body as it finds expression in the material world, which lives on and on in
those environs that have been created by what that soul
has seen and comprehended in its experience as being
according to those directions as He, the Father, the Lord
of all, would have each and every soul be.

⁵Then, as we find in the experiences of this entity,
these have become worthy attributes, as these are well
pleasing in His eyes; so that there may only be given that
injunction, "Be not weary in well-doing, for he that
endureth unto the end shall wear the crown of life." The
crown of life here means being aware of those abilities
within self to know that the self, the ego, the I, is in accord with, is aware of, the divine protection that has and
does come to each and every soul that fulfills its mission
in any experience.

⁶What, then, ye ask, has been the mission of this entity, this soul, in this experience? That, with that which
has gone before, there may be given the opportunity as

to what the soul would do about that it knows is in accordance with, in keeping with, what His injunctions have ever been to His fellow man; that ye make thy paths straight, that ye do unto thy fellow man as ye would have your fellow man do unto you; love the Lord thy God, eschewing evil, keeping the heart joyous in the service and in the tasks that are set before thee day by day, doing with a might in the Lord that thy hands find to do. For, His ways have ever been that ye grow in the grace and in the knowledge and in the understanding of the Lord and His ways. Not that ye rest idly by when there is work to do, but just being kind, just being patient, just being long-suffering with those who would err according to thine own conscience, yet in thine own life, in thine own dealings with such ye show forth that love, that patience that He hast shown with the sons of men since He has called into being *bodies*—physically—that are known in the material world that these may furnish a channel through which those things that are known and accepted as being the qualifications of a spiritual life may *find* manifestations, and thus bring forth their fruits, their meats, ready for repentance.

[7]For, while in humbleness of heart yet, in gladness does each soul find those things, those loads to be met day by day. And as there is the step taken here and there in the meditations (for, as He has given, "As oft as ye ask in my name, *believing*, it shall be done unto you"), He is faithful in His promises; for, as He has given, "I will not leave thee comfortless, but ye shall be quickened—even as the spirit in thee makes thee alive, makes thee aware of the joys that are thine through the service that thou may render to thy fellow man, in justness, in mercy, in just being kind, just being gentle to those here, there, that have become and do become thy lot to be measured with." For, there are no such things as perchance, but the law of demand, the law of supply, the laws of love are

ever, ever in thine own hands day by day. For, when there comes the needs that thou shouldst show forth thy love that has been shed on thee in thy activities in a material world, the opportunities that may be measured to thy fellow man are shown. For, as He has given, "Inasmuch as ye have done it unto the least of these, my little ones, ye have done it unto me."

[8]Hence, in thy steps, be acquainted with the Lord. Seek, in thy secret places, that He knoweth thee aright. And there will come those answers as thou meditatest in thine inner self as to what, where and how thou shalt measure thy steps day by day. For, justice and mercy and peace and harmony are as His gifts to those that seek His face. He has given, "If ye love me, keep my commandments." His commandments are not grievous, neither do they deny thee any influence, any material things that will make for joy in thine own experience. Rather do the fruits of mercy, peace, justice and harmony make for such in thine own experience.

[9]Hence, follow in the ways that are set before thee, knowing that He will call thee by name. And he that *He* names is redeemed in His sight. And there is nothing to fear save self. For, as has been given, "I am persuaded there is nothing in heaven, in earth, in principalities or in powers, that may separate the soul from the love of the Father save the waywardness, the indecisions, the unkindnesses that the self may inflict upon self or the fellow man."

[10]Keep the way. Feed His sheep. Tend His lambs, those that are in thy way, those thou meetest day by day. Let thine own light so shine that they may know that thou walkest, that thou talkest, oft with thy God.

[11]Ready for questions.

[12](Q) Is this entity one who may properly now pursue the higher and inner development of its soul and psychic forces?

(A) It is, as has been indicated. And in the development of the psychic forces, of the psychic influences and powers in the experience, enter into the Holy of Holies, cleansing the mind, the body, in whatsoever way and manner as prepareth or bespeaketh to thee that thou mayest present thyself in body and mind as being CLEAN and ready for the acceptance of that the Lord, thy God, may give thee in the way of directions. As He has promised to be thy guide, as He has sent His Son into the earth to show thee the way, be satisfied with nothing less than those that He may guide. Let thy prayer ever be:

Thy will, O God, be done in me as Thou seest I have need of, that I may be one with Thee—even as that I possessed with Thee before the world was.

[13](Q) Are the mental and physical bodies of this entity at war with each other in such a manner as to retard its soul and psychic development at the moment and, if so, in what manner and how best to overcome such condition?

(A) As indicated from that just given, such is not the condition. The way to meet all such, as has been indicated through these sources, is to seek in the mental mind the answer to all questions that may be presented in the things that may be thy experiences day by day, and have the answer within self as thou prayest. Then lay this answer before the Throne of grace, or mercy itself, as thou would meditate within the chambers of thine own heart, and the answer will be within self as to the necessary step, the necessary things to perform to be rid of the warring of the flesh with the spirit. While each body, each soul, in the flesh is subject to the flesh, yet—as has been given of Him, "Though ye may be in the world, ye may not be *of* this world, if ye will but put your whole trust, your whole love, your whole life, in His keeping." He will not lead thee astray. He will guide, guard and direct thee, even as has been given, "He loveth every one and giveth his own life for those that will come to Him."

In the preparations, then, for these warrings within, as has been given, meet them step by step. That that is given thee put to use, for only in the use of that which is thine own may this grow, even as patience and mercy and love and endurance and tolerance. Putting them to use they become those bulwarks that prevent an interception from carnal forces or the spirits of an evil influence. For, these are helpless in *His* sight; for He is made Lord of all.

[14](Q) Has this entity yet karmic debts from previous life experiences to be met and paid off. If so, briefly, of what nature and how best to be met with most benefit to others?

(A) Karmic influences must ever be met, but He has prepared a way that He takes them upon Himself, and as ye trust in Him He shows thee the way to meet the hindrances or conditions that would disturb thee in any phase of thine experience. For, karmic forces are: What is meted must be met. If they are met in Him that is the Maker, the Creator of all that exists in manifestation, as He has promised, then not in *blind* faith is it met—but by the deeds and the thoughts and the acts of the body, that through Him the conditions may be met day by day. Thus has He bought every soul that would trust in Him. For, since the foundations of the world He has paved the ways, here and there entering into the experience of man's existence that He may know every temptation that might beset man in all of his ways. Then in that as the Christ He came into the earth, fulfilling then that which makes Him that channel, that we making ourselves a channel through Him may—with the boldness of the Son—approach the Throne of mercy and grace and pardon, and know that all that has been done is washed away in that *He* has suffered that *we* have meted to our brother in the change that is wrought in our lives, through the manner we act toward him.

[15](Q) Has this entity yet karmic debts from previous life experiences to be met and paid off in regard to his immediate family? If so, briefly, of what nature and how best to be met with most benefit to them?

(A) No karmic debts from other sojourns or experiences enter in the present that may not be taken away in that, "Lord, have Thy ways with me. Use me as Thou seest fit that I may be one with Thee."

[16](Q) In the previous experiences given for this entity, his experiences seem to have been mostly in the economic fields. Why, then, has his present urge always been to express self through some form of art?

(A) Art and its higher meanings are meeting the economic influences in man in his every experience. That is easily seen by this entity, as it studies for the moment as to how that he has visualized God's glory in the earth and that man uses in his daily needs is but an expression of how those economic forces in the needs of the body of the man are blessed in their whole sense or terms.

Hence as the expression of this art in the soul of self to give expression to these very influences of nature itself that are the closest manifestations of the love of a merciful Father to a wayward son, it shows to the entity in his studies that these are but the expressions that may in their measures be meted to man in such a way and manner as may make him aware of the love of the Father. Not so much the obligation that man is to a merciful Father, but rather the privilege of the man in the presence of a merciful Father. Rather as the love of the man to the fellow man in the presence of Him who gives mercy and peace and life in all its phases in the experience of man, that he may but come to know His ways the better.

[17](Q) Had this entity any previous experiences on this earth during the Italian Renaissance period, or during

the Roman period, and if so, briefly, in what periods and
for what purpose?

(A) In both of these periods we find the activities of
the entity, rather in the one in the expression of the
physical forces of the body—in the Roman period—as in
the gladiator's activity; while in the Renaissance we find
rather the expression of self in—yes, some of the oils—
Reese (?)—Reese (?) is a portion of that assigned—in one
of the caves—now it's on a wall in—on a wall in a cave.
These expressions were to give, as it were, the combination of all the periods into one.

For the moment turn thy mind, my brother, to what
has been meant in the variations of manifestations in the
flesh, and in the spirit or in the soul body in its sojourn
in the environs of other spheres—where there are the
manifestations, as has oft been pointed out, of one particular activity; that is, one enters for a specific activity
in Mars, Mercury or Venus, and in Saturn for that cleansing that must come to all that have departed from the
earth and have not kept the ways clean. But in the earth
we find *all* rolled into one, with a body and a body-mind
for self-expression.

Hence, as has been given in regard to the appearances
and their associations with the economic forces and influences in the experiences of a people, so has the influence in the present brought to thine experience the
necessities of the activities in these directions; yet that
may be expressed in this material plane, this earth's activity, by self in those visualizations, in those activities in
the material things, in the meeting of the things in the
daily activities of life, that may find expression in *all* of
those things that may be found throughout the spheres.
For, as has been given by Him, "Other sheep I have that
are not of this fold," for they were on their journey that
they, too, might come and hear His voice, from His children and His brethren that would make known His ways.

What, ye ask again, are His ways? Just being kind, just being patient, just that as He gave, "A new commandment I give unto you, that ye love one another, that ye love thy neighbor as thyself, that *thou* would stand in thy neighbor's stead. Not to everyone that saith Lord, Lord, shall be called, but he that doeth the will of the Father." So in thine judgments, in the associations, he that doeth the will—or seeks to know the will, He may thy ways guide, He may thy acts manifested in His experience bring to the soul the knowledge of thy walks with thy God. Hence, as has been said, when thou prayest, let thy meditation be: "Use me, O God, as Thou seest I may better serve Thee; in my waking moments, in my walks and my dealings with my fellow man, be Thou the guide."

[18]We are through.

Chapter 5

PERSONALITY AND INDIVIDUALITY

READING 3590-2

As Edgar Cayce moved into the final years of his work, we see his spiritual psychology at its most mature level. Many of the readings given in this period were relatively short—in some instances due to the sheer workload that he had undertaken. But brevity is often the mark of wisdom, and some of these short readings are among his most important.

This reading, given only nine months before he had to discontinue his psychic work, is perhaps his most eloquent dissertation about personality and individuality. These two terms are the heart of the spiritual psychology that runs all through the readings. Don't expect to hear about this distinction if you take a college course in psychology, particularly from a professor who holds a mainstream point of view. Even in these last years of the twentieth century, it's still just an emergent perspective of the human mind and soul. Clearly Cayce was a pioneer in this effort fifty years ago.

The ideas in this reading are based on an assumption of lawfulness. The universe follows certain universal laws, just as the makeup of each one of us is purposefully and lawfully created. Paragraph 10 offers a helpful

analogy about the laws of our society, and it goes on to
refer to the way in which Jesus the Christ became an example for us of the right relationship between personality and individuality.

But what do these two terms mean? Paragraph 5 contains a succinct description of the personality. It's the self
that we present to the outside world. It resembles what
Jungian psychology calls the persona—the mask that
each of us wears and that we use to interact with the
people and situations of daily living. Our personality is
the familiar self-identity that we know. In an external
way, it's the self that we see in the mirror or the self that
we observe when watching a videotape of ourselves. But
it's *also* made up of certain elements of our *inner* lives.
For example, it can be observed in the familiar and rou-
tinized ways that we talk to ourselves silently. Those little
voices with which we second-guess ourselves or criticize
ourselves are likely to be aspects of the personality. They
are based on habit patterns we've learned along the way.

More often than not, the agenda of the personality is a
preoccupation with oneself and one's own importance—
what's referred to in paragraph 7 as the desire to have
other people "recognize your personal superiority." And
so we might think of the personality as starting from a
certain willfulness to put oneself at the center of things,
which in turn builds habits of thinking, feeling, and acting that begin to take on an automatic life of their own.

As noted in the description in paragraph 5, the personality can operate either consciously *or* unconsciously. Unfortunately, it's unconscious most of the
time. We tend to be on automatic pilot with our personality selves. Strong habit patterns drive us. The personality is the conditioned or ingrained element of our
being. It can be a formidable obstacle to our growth, especially when it tries to supplant the individuality.

The individuality is our more authentic being. It's the

self which has continuity from one lifetime to another. It's the higher self—a term that Cayce used only infrequently, preferring the term individuality, instead. Perhaps Cayce shied away from using the expression "higher self" because he did *not* want us to think of this deep and most authentic self as if it were already perfect. The individuality still needs to grow and develop. What makes it so special is its *capability* for growth and its strong *impetus* in that direction. (In contrast, the personality is often quite content with the status quo, even when that means some degree of discomfort or pain.)

The individuality-self is the identity that one awakens in meditation. In fact, one of Cayce's best definitions (281-13, Chapter 7) of this vital spiritual discipline is an activity which partakes not of the personality but instead of the individuality. You can probably remember times in your own meditation life when you felt yourself make that shift. Suddenly your habitual thinking and emotional patterns quieted down; and as they became still, you remembered another side of yourself. That freshly awakened aspect of yourself was in touch with "universal consciousness" (see paragraph 7) and most likely it felt clear and strong. Connecting with your individuality probably made you feel secure and safe, so that it was easy to offer heartfelt prayers for other people at the end of the meditation session.

At the most basic level, what makes these two sides of us different? How is the personality-self unlike this more genuine way of knowing ourselves? The essential distinction is one of perspective and worldview. It's beautifully illustrated in Cayce's example of Jim, John, and Susan (in paragraphs 5 and 6). Our personality-selves think, say, and do things with a very specific motivational point of view: our own needs. On the other hand, our individuality-selves can look at the same situations or opportunities with a different motivational perspective: concern for the *greater good* and an ability to honor the *needs of others*. Essentially this is the Golden Rule, alluded to in paragraph 6.

Admittedly, all this makes the personality sound pretty bad and the individuality pretty wonderful. However, in other readings about this subject, Cayce reminds us that the personality is a necessary element to living in a body in the material world. To a certain extent we need to look out for ourselves and even to develop some habits and routines. (Can you imagine driving a car and having to be constantly attentive to every little thing you do? Here, the personality serves a very useful purpose.) A big problem, however, arises when we lose touch with the individuality and mistakenly believe that the personality-self is all there is to us.

Working with ideals is the key to staying clear about the distinction and to keeping in touch with your individuality-self. In fact, the last half of this reading contains specific instructions about the questions you can ask yourself in order to determine your ideals—spiritually, mentally, and physically. By knowing what we believe in and what we hold as core values, we have a simple and direct way to call the individuality-self back to awareness. The heart of walking a spiritual path is found in those little choices—potentially made dozens of times a day—to resist the habitual tug of personality and listen to the wisdom of the individuality.

THE READING

This psychic reading, 3590-2, was given by Edgar Cayce on January 26, 1944. The conductor was Gertrude Cayce.

[1]GC: You will give a mental and spiritual reading for this entity, with information, advice and guidance that will be helpful at this time; answering the questions, that may be asked:

[2]EC: Yes, we have the body, the inquiring mind, [3590].

[3]In giving that which may be helpful for this entity, as we find, many of the conditions that are as personalities and individualities are to be considered.

[4]Here, for the entity, personality and individuality should have some analysis, so as to give the entity a concept of what we mean by personality and individuality:

[5]Personality is that which the entity, consciously or unconsciously, spreads out before others to be seen of others. As to whether you will say Good Morning to Jim or John, and ignore Susan or not—these are parts of the personality, because of some difference or because of some desire to be used or needed by *that* others would have to give.

[6]While individuality in that same circumstance would be: I wish to do this or that for Susan or Jim or John, because I would like for Jim or John or Susan to do this if conditions were reversed.

[7]One is for the universal consciousness that is part of the soul-entity's activity. The other is the personal, or the desire for recognition, or the desire for the other individual to recognize your personal superiority.

[8]These are variations to this individual entity.

[9]Then, in analyzing the mental and spiritual influences as may be applicable in the experience, the entity finds itself—if it will stop to analyze—a body, a mind, with the hope for a soul eternal, that will constantly, eter-

nally have recognition of those relationships to the universal consciousness or God.

[10]Then, as the entity in this material plane has found, it is necessary physically to conform to certain moral and penal laws of society, of the state, of the nation, even to be termed a good citizen. Thus if there is to be preparation for the entity as the soul-entity, as a citizen of the heavenly kingdom, isn't it just as necessary that there be conforming to the laws pertaining to that spiritual kingdom of which the entity is a part? And there has been an ensample, a citizen of that kingdom, the Son Himself, has given the example to the entity as well as to others. Isn't it well, then, that the entity study to show self approved unto that kingdom, rightly putting the proper emphasis upon all phases of His admonitions, His judgments, His commandments, and thus become such an one as to be a good citizen of that individual kingdom?

[11]These are just reasons within self, if there is the time taken to interpret what ye believe and what ye hope for.

[12]Do not do it just mentally. Do it mentally and materially. Set it down in three distinct columns: The physical—what are the attributes of the physical body? Eyes, ears, nose, mouth—these are means or manners through which the awarenesses of the physical body may become known to others, by sight, by hearing, by speaking, by feeling, by smelling. These are consciousnesses. Then there are the emotions of the body. These come under the mental heading, yes—but there are also those phases where the mental and emotional body is born, or under the control of the physical and sometimes under the control wholly of the mental. What are the mental attributes, then? The ability to think, the ability to act upon thought. From whence do these arise? Do you use the faculties of the physical being for such? You do in many instances, yet you can think by sitting still—you can think yourself wherever your consciousness has made an impression

upon the physical being of what exists. For you can sit in your office and see yourself at home, and know exactly what your bed looks like and what you left set under it when you left this morning! These are physical, not material at all; yet you judge them by paralleling with that knowledge, that understanding.

[13]The spiritual self is life, the activity of the mental and of the physical is of the soul—and thus a soul-body.

[14]Set down the attributes of each, and as to when and how you use them, and how you change them. What is the ideal of each? Of your mental, your physical and your spiritual or soul body? And as you grow in grace, we will find that the individuality will change—until you become one, as the Father and the Son and the Holy Spirit are one.

[15]This is the manner in which you grow.

[16]Then study to show thyself approved unto God, a workman not ashamed, rightly dividing the words of truth, keeping self unspotted from the world; not condemning, even as ye would not be condemned. For as ye pray, as He taught, "Forgive me as I forgive others." So in thy condemning, so in thy passing judgment, let it be only as ye would be judged by thy Maker.

[17]We are through for the present.

Chapter 6

THE PSYCHOLOGY OF IDEALS

READING 357-13

Anyone who has studied the Cayce readings knows how important ideals are—if for no other reason than how often they are mentioned. Perhaps you've encountered these and other examples: The approach to meditation advocated in the readings is ideals centered. One of Cayce's most innovative dream interpretation strategies is to measure what's happening in your dream against the ideals that you hold. And the philosophy of healing rests on having an ideal and a purpose for wanting to get well.

The most-quoted Cayce passage about ideals comes from this reading for a forty-year-old woman, [357], working as a clerk during World War II. "Then, the more important, the most important experience of this or any individual entity is to first know what *is* the ideal—spiritually." But lots more than just this one highly quotable claim makes reading 357-13 special. In fact, the entire reading is universally valuable because it points to how ideals work in our lives, and it outlines the spiritual ideal that Cayce's source held in highest esteem: the universal Christ.

As you study this reading, first notice how Cayce describes (in paragraphs 3 and 4) the essential human dilemma. Our minds—with extraordinary creative potential—are pulled in two directions. On the one hand is the attraction of an ideal, a positive, creative image of what is possible. In contrast there is the tug of material desires. Unfortunately it's those limiting, destructive influences that frequently gain the upper hand.

How do those desires which are focused on materiality gain our attention? Usually it's either by (1) crises and emergencies or (2) good excuses and rationalizations. Think about your own life in those terms. What interrupts or diverts you; what interferes with the pursuit of your ideals? For most of us, it's an endless stream of material life demands that seem too important to ignore. In these stressful modern times, almost everyone has days that seem to be ruled by crises or emergencies.

The second attention diverter is a frequent impulse to say or do something that seems justifiable in the moment. In those instances, simply because we can rationalize it, we settle for something less than our best.

See if you can remember personal examples from the past twenty-four hours—instances in which diversions or detours took you away from your ideal. This exercise isn't meant to make you feel guilty. It's merely a matter of seeing just how commonplace is the process that Cayce describes.

Of course, merely recognizing this aspect of the psychology of ideals still leaves unanswered one vital question: "What is the best ideal for us to hold?" Clearly the Cayce readings have in mind a specific spiritual ideal as the optimum. In the language of the readings, it is the universal Christ. It was demonstrated and lived by Jesus. Just as significantly, it's a seed-like pattern in each one of us. This reading contains one of Cayce's most eloquent descriptions of that universal Christ pattern, beginning with paragraph 9.

What happens in us when we make a commitment to that pattern as our personal ideal? Or for that matter, what happens when we invest ourselves in any ideal? The setting of a spiritual ideal engages forces in the unconscious mind that can dramatically alter our lives. That's exactly why Cayce called it the most important experience that a soul can have.

But precisely what does it mean to "set a spiritual ideal"? Is it just a matter of telling someone else what you've done, or of writing it down on a piece of paper? In reading 357-13, two crucial elements are alluded to. These two ingredients are central to the psychology of ideals. Both aspects play a role whereby the forces of soul, lying dormant in the unconscious mind, are stirred to life. Both involve an act of free will and an engagement of the creative mind.

Aspiration is the first ingredient in Cayce's psychology of ideals. To hold the universal Christ as a spiritual ideal means to aspire to its qualities. (Much of reading 357-13 is an inspirational message encouraging this woman to aspire to such an ideal.) Maybe those qualities seem out of reach, but we can feel ourselves inwardly stretching and reaching for all that the Christ Consciousness means to us. The same would hold true for any other spiritual ideal chosen. What's most important to understanding the psychology of ideals is that the striving involves both the will and the creative side of the mind. We have to make the choice, *and* we need to use the imaginative forces to shape a relationship to that possibility for ourselves.

It probably comes as no surprise that "aspiration" is one of the two key ingredients in Cayce's view of how ideals work. Just think about how people use the word "ideal" in everyday language. It usually has the flavor of aspiration. For example, the ideal home situation is something that we can creatively imagine as the very best possible way of getting along with our family members. The ideal job is an imagined workplace situation that we long to have because all of our talents would be used.

Trust is the second ingredient in Cayce's psychology of ideals (paragraph 14). This is a more subtle factor than aspiration. Think about how you might aspire to something but not trust that it's really alive within you, not trust that it's possible to experience for yourself. Without investing yourself through trust, you haven't yet set a spiritual ideal.

This may not be a point of view that's easy to swallow, simply because most of us find trusting to be very difficult. To trust requires a more challenging use of free will than does aspiration alone. Trust means a willingness to surrender and let go of fears and doubts. It means to place ultimate belief in forces beyond our personal conscious selves. According to this perspective, you haven't yet set the universal Christ—or anything else—as your spiritual ideal until you let go and put your trust in it.

Think about a somewhat superficial example—one that allows a quick remembrance of what it feels like to trust. When you turn on a light, you trust that the electricity will be there, ready to light up the room. When you turn the handle on the faucet, you trust that the water will start flowing. In other words, you spend little of your day worrying about the availability of power and water. Now, of course, a critic could say that you're mindlessly taking it all for granted—that many people in the world don't have immediate access to these resources. But the point isn't how fortunate we are. These examples teach us something about trust—something that is related to trusting an ideal.

The authentic ideal you hold is the one you don't have to spend time thinking about or questioning. It has become so much a part of your life that it's a "given." When you meet a difficulty or a challenge, you know you can count on the inspiration and power of that ideal just as surely as you count on electricity and water when you need them. Some days your genuine ideal has the quality of being almost invisible to you because it's so deeply a part of how you look at the world. It's so essential that you don't stop to question it or worry about it. You can take it for granted.

In the 1990s we live in an era that deeply needs a renewed vision of the power of ideals. Not pie-in-the-sky idealism. That too often fails to make the connection with practical life. What's so badly required in today's world is respect (even reverence) for that crucial step called "setting an ideal for one's own individual life." Cayce's spiritual psychology offers one very effective way to hone in on exactly how to do it and make it work. Vivid aspiration is one key; the other is the courage to trust.

THE READING

This psychic reading, 357-13, was given by Edgar Cayce on June 11, 1942. The conductor was Gertrude Cayce.

[1]GC: You will have before you the body and inquiring mind of [357], at ... Jewelry Co., ..., Va., in regard to her health, her home life, her work, and her general welfare. You will give a mental and spiritual reading, with information, advice and guidance that will be helpful; answering the questions she has submitted, as I ask them:

[2]EC: In giving an interpretation of the physical, mental and spiritual well-being of a body, in terms of a mental and spiritual reading—as we have so oft indicated, Mind is the Builder.

[3]The mind uses its spiritual ideals to build upon. And the mind also uses the material desires as the destructive channels, or it is the interference by the material

desires that prevents a body and a mind from keeping in perfect accord with its ideal.

⁴Thus, these continue ever in the material plane to be as warriors one with another. Physical emergencies or physical conditions may oft be used as excuses, or as justifications for the body choosing to do this or that.

⁵Ought these things so to be, according to thy ideal?

⁶Then, the more important, the most important experience of this or any individual entity is to first know what *is* the ideal—spiritually.

⁷Who and what is thy pattern?

⁸Throughout the experience of man in the material world, at various seasons and periods, teachers or "would be" teachers have come; setting up certain forms or certain theories as to manners in which an individual shall control the appetites of the body or of the mind, so as to attain to some particular phase of development.

⁹There has also come a teacher who was bold enough to declare himself as the son of the living God. He set no rules of appetite. He set no rules of ethics, other than "As ye would that men should do to you, do ye even so to them," and to know "Inasmuch as ye do it unto the least of these, thy brethren, ye do it unto thy Maker." He declared that the kingdom of heaven is within each individual entity's consciousness, to be attained, to be aware of—through meditating upon the fact that God is the Father of every soul.

¹⁰Jesus, the Christ, is the mediator. And in Him, and in the study of His examples in the earth, is *life*—and that ye may have it more abundantly. He came to demonstrate, to manifest, to give life and light to all.

¹¹Here, then, ye find a friend, a brother, a companion. As He gave, "I call ye not servants, but brethren." For, as many as believe, to them He gives power to become the children of God, the Father; joint heirs with this Jesus, the Christ, in the knowledge and in the awareness of this

presence abiding ever with those who set this ideal before them.

¹²What, then, is this as an ideal?

¹³As concerning thy fellow man, He gave, "As ye would that others do to you, do ye even so to them," take no thought, worry not, be not overanxious about the body. For He knoweth what ye have need of. In the place thou art, in the consciousness in which ye find yourself, is that which is *today, now,* needed for thy greater, thy better, thy more wonderful unfoldment.

¹⁴But today *hear* His voice, "Come unto me, all that are weak or that are heavy-laden, and I will give you rest from those worries, peace from those anxieties." For the Lord loveth those who put their trust *wholly* in Him.

¹⁵This, then, is that attitude of mind that puts away hates, malice, anxiety, jealousy. And it creates in their stead, in that Mind is the Builder, the fruits of the spirit— love, patience, mercy, long-suffering, kindness, gentleness. And these—against such there is no law. They break down barriers, they bring peace and harmony, they bring the outlook upon life of not finding fault because someone "forgot," someone's judgment was bad, someone was selfish today. These ye can overlook, for so did He.

¹⁶In His own experience with those that He had chosen out of the world, if He had held disappointment in their leaving Him to the mercies of an indignant high priest, a determined lawyer and an unjust steward, what would have been *thy* hope, thy promise today?   .

¹⁷For He, though with the ability to destroy, thought not of such but rather gave Himself; that the Creative Forces, God, might be reconciled to that pronouncement, that judgment. And thus mercy, through the shedding of blood, came into man's experience.

Chapter 7

MEDITATION

READING 281-13

In this discourse there are at least three central noteworthy themes—definitions that allow us to distinguish prayer from meditation, the importance of cleansing, and the technique of engaging the imaginative forces as a kind of transformed thinking.

Several definitions of meditation are offered, including one near the end of the reading that has frequently been quoted (i.e., "*emptying* self of all that hinders the creative forces from rising"). But perhaps the most useful one is embedded in this reading and could easily be overlooked because it's not directly announced as a definition: Meditation partakes of the individuality, not the personality.

Personality is our normal physical consciousness—our likes and dislikes, our agendas of things to be accomplished, and our habit patterns. (See Chapter 5.) It's the familiar sense of identity that each of us holds—or we might say, holds us. And prayer is largely an activity of that personality-self. It's a special effort made by the personality, the "pouring out of the personality" so that we can be filled. "Prayer is the concerted effort of the physical consciousness . . ."

On the other hand, meditation requires that this personality-self become still. Meditation is an emptying; it is a cessation of thinking—even high-minded thinking—as we typically experience it. It involves the awakening and engagement of this other side of our being: individuality. This is the word used most often in the Cayce readings for our own higher self. It is an aspect of us that is still evolving and developing, yet is more immediately connected to the spiritual world.

What is the *language* of individuality? How does it operate in meditation? This Cayce reading suggests that the key is in the imaginative forces. We are transformed in meditation by holding in attention and raising within ourselves a certain quality of image. Actual *creation* takes place; or we might say that in meditation we are being "re-created." Near the end of the reading a very clear statement is made concerning the nature of that image: the Christ (although it's evident that what is intended here is the universal Christ Consciousness since it's equated with "love of God").

One secret to effective meditation is therefore the ability to stop normal thinking processes and to imaginatively hold a very high ideal in one's attention. This imaginative activity does not mean daydreaming (as the companion reading 281-41 points out), but is a way of perceiving and experiencing the reality of that ideal with one's feelings and intuitions. Our sense of self moves "deeper—deeper—to the seeing, feeling, experiencing of that image in the creative forces of love . . . "

Another key to effective meditation, according to this reading, is obviously *cleansing.* Almost half the text deals with this subject from one angle or another. Why is the purification of our bodies and our minds so significant? One reason why so much information was given on cleansing probably goes back to the suggestive request recited to Mr. Cayce as the reading began. They were looking for advice on how to meditate "without the effort disturbing the mental or physical body." The way to minimize the likelihood of any disturbance is cleansing in advance.

But another rationale for purification is also proposed in the discourse. That reason is based on the model of what happens as we hold our ideal in silent attention without imaginative forces. The influence and vibration of that image rises within the body through the spiritual centers (or chakras). It moves from the reproductive center and cells of Leydig all the way up to the pineal and pituitary centers in the brain.

What can limit how high that image can be raised? This particular reading identifies two factors. If we have abused our mental forces and can only imagine a very limited ideal, then the movement of that image is greatly restricted. It won't resonate to the higher centers and simply won't go that far. The other limitation, however, can easily be present even if we've honed in on the Christ ideal. Impurities in our physical or mental bodies constitute something against which this image has to work in the effort to disseminate itself to "these centers, stations or places along the body." They become resistive hindrances.

Of course, this is not an all-or-nothing proposition. If we waited until we were totally purified before trying to meditate, we might never get around to it. Cleansing, like effective meditation itself, has levels. The point is simply to do what we can before we start to meditate, in order to minimize these hindering factors, and the reading gives several possible methods.

In summary, this remarkable reading is valuable to any of us who are motivated to include meditation in our daily life style. The beginner will discover here a straightforward approach. And the experienced meditator will undoubtedly find this reading worthy of repeated study.

It captures the essential themes of this vital spiritual discipline.

THE READING

This psychic reading, 281-13, was given by Edgar Cayce on November 19, 1932. The conductor was Gertrude Cayce.

[1]GC: You will have before you the psychic work of Edgar Cayce, present in this room, the information that has been and is being given from time to time, especially that regarding meditation and prayer. You will give, in a clear, concise, understandable manner just how an individual may meditate, or pray, without the effort disturbing the mental or physical body. If this can be given in a general manner, outline it for us. If it is necessary to be outlined for specific individuals, you will tell us how individuals may attain to the understanding necessary for such experiences not to be detrimental to them.

[2]EC: Yes, we have the work, the information that has been and that maybe given from time to time; especially that in reference to meditation and prayer.

[3]First, in considering such, it would be well to analyze that difference (that is not always understood) between meditation and prayer.

[4]As it has been defined or given in an illustrated manner by the Great Teacher, prayer is the *making* of one's conscious self more in attune with the spiritual forces that may manifest in a material world, and is *ordinarily* given as a *cooperative* experience of *many* individuals when all are asked to come in one accord and one mind; or, as was illustrated by:

[5]Be not as the Pharisees, who love to be seen of men, who make long dissertation or prayer to be heard of men. They *immediately* have their reward in the physical-mental mind.

⁶Be rather as he that entered the temple and not so much as lifting his eyes, smote his breast and said, "God, be merciful to me a sinner!"

⁷Which man was justified, this man or he that stood to be seen of men and thanked God he was not as other men, that he paid his tithes, that he did the services required in the temple, that he stood in awe of no one, he was not even as this heathen who in an uncouth manner, not with washed hands, not with shaven face attempted to reach the throne of grace?

⁸Here we have drawn for us a comparison in prayer: That which may be the pouring out of the personality of the individual, or a group who enter in for the purpose of either outward show to be seen of men; or that enter in even as in the closet of one's inner self and pours out self that the inner man may be filled with the Spirit of the Father in His merciful kindness to men.

⁹Now draw the comparisons for meditation: Meditation, then, is prayer, but is prayer from *within* the *inner* self, and partakes not only of the physical inner man but the soul that is aroused by the spirit of man from within.

¹⁰Well, that we consider this from *individual* interpretation, as well as from group interpretation; or individual meditation and group meditation.

¹¹As has been given, there are *definite* conditions that arise from within the inner man when an individual enters into true or deep meditation. A physical condition happens, a physical activity takes place! Acting through what? Through that man has chosen to call the imaginative or the impulsive, and the sources of impulse are aroused by the shutting out of thought pertaining to activities or attributes of the carnal forces of man. That is true whether we are considering it from the group standpoint or the individual. Then, changes naturally take place when there is the arousing of that stimuli *within* the individual that has within it the seat of the soul's

dwelling, within the individual body of the entity or man, and then this partakes of the individuality rather than the personality.

[12]If there has been set the mark (mark meaning here the image that is raised by the individual in its imaginative and impulse force) such that it takes the form of the ideal the individual is holding as its standard to be raised to, within the individual as well as to all forces and powers that are magnified or to be magnified in the world from without, *then* the individual (or the image) bears the mark of the Lamb, or the Christ, or the Holy One, or the Son, or any of the names we may have given to that which *enables* the individual to enter *through it* into the very presence of that which is the creative force from within itself—see?

[13]Some have so overshadowed themselves by abuses of the mental attributes of the body as to make scars, rather than the mark, so that only an imperfect image may be raised within themselves that may rise no higher than the arousing of the carnal desires within the individual body. We are speaking individually, of course; we haven't raised it to where it may be disseminated, for remember it rises from the glands known in the body as the lyden, or to the lyden [Leydig] and through the reproductive forces themselves, which are the very essence of Life itself within an individual—see? for these functionings never reach that position or place that they do not continue to secrete that which makes for virility to an individual physical body. Now we are speaking of conditions from without and from within!

[14]The spirit and the soul is within its encasement, or its temple within the body of the individual—see? With the arousing then of this image, it rises along that which is known as the Appian Way, or the pineal center, to the base of the *brain*, that it may be disseminated to those centers that give activity to the whole of the mental and

physical being. It rises then to the hidden eye in the center of the brain system, or is felt in the forefront of the head, or in the place just above the real face—or bridge of nose, see?

[15]Do not be confused by the terms that we are necessarily using to give the exact location of the activities of these conditions within the individuals, that we may make this clarified for individuals.

[16]When an individual then enters into deep meditation:

[17]It has been found throughout the ages (*individuals* have found) that self-preparation (to *them*) is necessary. To some it is necessary that the body be cleansed with pure water, that certain types of breathing are taken, that there may be an even balance in the whole of the respiratory system, that the circulation becomes normal in its flow through the body, that certain or definite odors produce those conditions (or are conducive to producing of conditions) that allay or stimulate the activity of portions of the system, that the more carnal or more material sources are laid aside, or the whole of the body is *purified* so that the purity of thought as it rises has less to work against in its dissemination of that it brings to the whole of the system, in its rising through the whole of these centers, stations or places along the body. To be sure, these are conducive; as are also certain incantations, as a drone of certain sounds, as the tolling of certain tones, bells, cymbals, drums, or various kinds of skins. Though we may as higher thought individuals find some fault with those called savages, they produce or arouse or bring within themselves—just as we have known, do know, that there may be raised through the battle-cry, there may be raised through the using of certain words or things, the passion or the thirst for destructive forces. Just the same may there be raised, not sedative to these but a *cleansing* of the body.

[18]"Consecrate yourselves this day that ye may on the morrow present yourselves before the Lord that He may speak through *you!*" is not amiss. So, to *all* there may be given:

[19]*Find* that which is to *yourself* the more certain way to your consciousness of *purifying* body and mind, before ye attempt to enter into the meditation as to raise the image of that through which ye are seeking to know the will or the activity of the Creative Forces; for ye are *raising* in meditation actual *creation* taking place within the inner self!

[20]When one has found that which to self cleanses the body, whether from the keeping away from certain foods or from certain associations (either man or woman), or from those thoughts and activities that would hinder that which is to be raised from *finding* its full measure of expression in the *inner* man (*inner* man, or inner individual, man or woman, meaning in this sense those radial senses from which, or centers from which all the physical organs, the mental organs, receive their stimuli for activity), we readily see how, then, *in* meditation (when one has so purified self) that *healing* of *every* kind and nature may be disseminated on the wings of thought, that are so much a thing—and so little considered by the tongue that speaks without taking into consideration what may be the end thereof!

[21]Now, when one has cleansed self, in whatever manner it may be, there may be no fear that it will become so overpowering that it will cause any physical or mental disorder. It is *without* the cleansing that entering any such finds *any* type or form of disaster, or of pain, or of any dis-ease of any nature. It is when the thoughts, then, or when the cleansings of *group* meditations are conflicting that such meditations call on the higher forces raised within self for manifestations and bring those conditions that either draw one closer to another or

make for that which shadows [shatters?] much in the experiences of others; hence short group meditations with a *central* thought around some individual idea, or either in words, incantations, or by following the speech of one sincere in abilities, efforts or desires to raise a cooperative activity *in* the minds, would be the better.

[22]Then, as one formula—not the only one, to be sure—for an individual that would enter into meditation for self, for others:

[23]Cleanse the body with pure water. Sit or lie in an easy position, without binding garments about the body. Breathe in through the right nostril three times, and exhale through the mouth. Breathe in three times through the left nostril and exhale through the right. Then, either with the aid of a low music, or the incantation of that which carries self deeper—deeper—to the seeing, feeling, experiencing of that image in the creative forces of love, enter into the Holy of Holies. As self feels or experiences the raising of this, see it disseminated through the *inner* eye (not the carnal eye) to that which will bring the greater understanding in meeting every condition in the experience of the body. Then listen to the music that is made as each center of thine own body responds to that new creative force that little by little this entering in will enable self to renew all that is necessary—in Him.

[24]First, *cleanse* the room; cleanse the body; cleanse the surroundings, in thought, in act! Approach not the inner man, or the inner self, with a grudge or an unkind thought held against *any* man! or do so to thine own undoing sooner or later!

[25]Prayer and meditation:

[26]Prayer is the concerted effort of the physical consciousness to become attuned to the consciousness of the Creator, either collectively or individually! *Meditation* is *emptying* self of all that hinders the creative forces from rising along the natural channels of the physical

man to be disseminated through those centers and sources that create the activities of the physical, the mental, the spiritual man; properly done must make one *stronger* mentally, physically, for has it not been given? ·He went in the strength of that meat received for many days? Was it not given by Him who has shown us the Way, "I have had meat that ye know not of"? As we give out, so does the *whole* of man—physically and mentally become depleted, yet in entering into the silence, entering into the silence in meditation, with a clean hand, a clean body, a clean mind, we may receive that strength and power that fits each individual, each soul, for a greater activity in this material world.

[27]"Be not afraid, it is I." Be sure it is Him we worship that we raise in our inner selves for the dissemination; for, as He gave, "Ye must eat of my *body;* ye must drink of *my* blood." Raising then in the inner self that image of the Christ, love of the God Consciousness, is *making* the body so cleansed as to be barred against all powers that would in any manner hinder.

[28]Be thou *clean,* in Him.

[29]We are through for the present.

Chapter 8

Spiritual Advice

READING 987-4

The mental-spiritual readings contain some of the best and most generally useful information given by Edgar Cayce. While not as well known as the physical health readings with their holistic strategy for healing or the life readings with their remarkable story of how reincarnation works, the mental-spiritual readings are a gold mine of principle and concepts for the spiritual life. This one is a good example. The messages it contains for this forty-nine-year-old housewife are relevant for any seeker.

At least two features make it noteworthy. First is its treatment of the elusive question of personal identity. What is the ego-self as opposed to the spiritual-self? What does it mean to be selfish? Second, this reading is one of the finest and most direct statements from Cayce about the importance of ideals, purposes, and motives. For example, the very purpose of life is described as the opportunity to choose a spiritual ideal. Something deep within our souls is at work when we make decisions about values and intentions. It is the "spiritual self" in action that we feel and experience whenever we turn our minds to such questions.

The key point here seems to be that the "soul seeks expression." Its natural impulse is not to remain hidden but to reveal itself. For [987], this occurred as "soul visions" that spontaneously arose while she was meditating. By "the centers becoming attuned"—that is, by the chakras or spiritual centers harmonizing their activity—her mind would break through the maze of confusion and catch a clear glimpse of a higher truth. We might well ask how that same process is at work in our own lives. In what setting are we most likely to experience the soul self that continually seeks expression?

This reading frequently refers to personal identity—whether it's the ego, the "I AM," the spiritual self, or other expressions. The reading tries to help us sort out answers to some ancient questions:

Who am I, really? From day to day—even from hour to hour—I seem to change the feeling of who I am.

How can my limited, egocentric self ever be reconciled to the unlimited higher self which also lives in me?

Cayce's answer is profound yet subtle: identity is linked to the realm of intentions. Change your intention—your motive, purpose, or ideal—and your sense of yourself alters.

This powerful concept is subtle because we can easily mistake what is meant by the word "intent." It's deeper than a momentary whim and more significant than such casual comments as "I intend to mow the lawn this weekend." A quality of human experience much bigger than simply making plans is addressed here. Cayce means something akin to what theologians call "intentionality," which resides at the core of our *values*. It has both a conscious and an unconscious aspect; it has both a mental outlook and a will to application (what this reading calls "the beauty of the inner life lived").

Our sense of self is largely shaped by this deep undercurrent of outlook. One's fundamental, spiritual ideal has a measure of permanence, or at least is slow to change. It's not the sort of thing that you change every day, such as your clothing. The choosing—and living—of a spiritual ideal, in the way Cayce is speaking of it here, is a *lifetime* work. It's a task so significant that it is the very purpose of our incarnation. Intentionality—or what this reading calls purposes and intents—takes a long time and considerable discipline to change. But the stakes are high. If we choose properly, then the spiritual self slowly becomes the conscious self.

What then do we have to choose from? What quality of intentionality can we adopt? To simplify matters, the selection is between two polar opposites. On the one hand there is what this reading calls "self intent," and on the other, the intent of service and compassion that leads us to become "the saving grace to someone." That higher kind of intent—that intentionality of the soul—includes both the components of understanding and action.

How can we know when we've slipped from that higher ideal back into the more limited one? One clue is given: the meaning of the ego-self is the taking of offense. It takes hindrances personally so that they hurt oneself. Countless variations on this theme all boil down to the same thing: putting one's own feelings first.

What's the remedy? The key is proposed here, stated with the rhetorical question, "For what is the gain if ye love those *only* that love thee?" In other words, it's possible to adopt an outlook on life—an intentionality or ideal—that does *not use worldly standards of fairness* as the ultimate. There is a deeper ethic that might seem illogical, one that offers peace in the face of violence and responds with joy to despair. Admittedly, it's not easy to live that way. Some days we don't even want to try. But that's why we're given a long time to work on it.

This, and only this, leads to enlightened awareness and

spiritual freedom; not special diets, consciousness-alter-
ing techniques, secret mantras, or astrological insights.
Sometimes these small tools can help. But what it really
comes down to—as Jesus, the Buddha, Gandhi, and others have demonstrated—is that in the smallest of human
interactions we make the biggest statements about our
values and ideals, even about the level of our own spirituality.

THE READING

*This psychic reading, 987-4, was given by Edgar Cayce
on November 2, 1937. The conductor was Gertrude Cayce.*

[1]GC: You will have before you the entity, [987], present
in this room, who seeks a mental and spiritual reading,
with information, advice and guidance as to her development and proper expression in the earth. You will answer the questions she submits, as I ask them:

[2]EC: Yes, we have the entity, [987].

[3]In giving the analysis of the mental and spiritual self,
many are the conditions that arise as questions in the
experience of the entity. These to be sure must be approached as to the purpose and the desires of the *spiritual* self.

[4]That there may be a more perfect understanding,
much as to those that have been the experiences of the
entity as a soul-entity must be referred to.

[5]For, life—or the motivative force of a soul—is eternal;
and that portion of same that is motivated by the mental
and spiritual attributes of an entity has experienced,
does experience the influences that have guided or
prompted same through its sojourns.

[6]For each soul seeks expression. And as it moves
through the mental associations and attributes in the
surrounding environs, it gives out that which becomes

either for selfish reactions of the own ego—to express—
or for the I AM to be at-one with the Great I AM THAT I
AM.

[7]What then are the purposes for the activities of an
entity in a material plane, surrounded with those environs that make for self-expressions or self-activities in
the various ways and manners?

[8]What meaneth these? That self is growing to that
which it, the entity, the soul, is to present, as it were, to
the Great I AM in those experiences when it is absent
from materiality.

[9]These become hard at times for the individual to vi-
sualize; that the mental and soul may manifest without
a physical vehicle. Yet in the deeper meditations, in those
experiences when those influences may arise when the
spirit of the Creative Force, the universality of soul, of
mind—not as material, not as judgments, not *in* time
and space but *of* time and space—may become lost in
the Whole, instead of the entity being lost in the maze of
confusing influences—then the soul visions arise in the
meditations.

[10]And the centers becoming attuned to the vibrations
of the bodily force, these give a vision of that as may be
to the entity an outlet for the self-expressions, in the
beauties and the harmonies and the activities that become, in their last analysis; just being patient, long-suffering, gentle, kind. *These* are the fruits of the spirit of
truth; just as hates, malice and the like become in their
growths those destructive forces in creating, in making
for those things that are as but tares, confusions, dissen-
sions in the experiences of an entity.

[11]Those then are the purposes of the entrance of an
entity into a material plane; to choose that which is its
ideal.

[12]Then ask thyself the question—gain the answer first
in thy physical consciousness:

[13]"What is my ideal of a *spiritual* life?"

[14]Then when the answer has come—for it has been given by Him that is Life, that the kingdom of God, the kingdom of heaven, is within; and we view the kingdom of God without by the application of those things that are of the spirit of truth—These then answered, ye seek again in the inner consciousness:

[15]"Am I true to my ideal?"

[16]These become then the answers. This and that and the other; never as pro and con. For the growth in the spirit is as He has given; ye *grow* in grace, in knowledge, in understanding.

[17]How? As ye would have mercy shown thee, ye show mercy to those that even despitefully use thee. If ye would be forgiven for that which is contrary to thy own purposes—yet through the vicissitudes of the experiences about thee, anger and wrath give place to better judgment—ye, too, will forgive those that have despitefully used thee; ye will hold no malice. For ye would that thy Ideal, that Way ye seek, hold no malice—yea, no judgment—against thee. For it is the true law of recompense; yea, the true law of sacrifice.

[18]For not in sacrifice alone has He sought His judgments, but rather in mercy, in grace, in fortitude; yea, in divine love.

[19]The shadows of these are seen in thy inner experience with thy fellow man day by day. For ye have seen a smile, yea a kind word, turn away wrath. Ye have seen a gentleness give hope to those that have lost their hold on purpose, other than the satisfying of an appetite—yea, other than satisfying the desires of the carnal mind.

[20]Hence as ye give, ye receive. For this is mercy, this is grace. This is the beauty of the inner life lived.

[21]Know then it is not that judgment is passed here or there. For know that God looketh upon the heart and He judgeth rather the purposes, the desires, the intents.

²²For what seekest thou to lord (laud) in thy life? Self intent? Know ye not that it was selfishness that separated the souls from the spirit of life and light? Then only in the divine love do ye have the opportunity to become to thy fellow man a saving grace, a mercy, yea even a savior.

²³For until ye have in thy own material associations known thyself to be the saving grace to someone, ye may not know even the whole mercy of the Father with the children of men.

²⁴Then it is not of rote; it is not ritual that has made for those influences in thine own experience; but in whom, in what hast thou put thy trust?

²⁵He has promised to meet thee within the temple of thine own body. For as has been given, thy body is the temple of the living God; a tabernacle, yea, for thy soul. And in the holy of holies within thine own consciousness He may walk and talk with thee.

²⁶How? How?

²⁷Is it the bringing of sacrifice? Is it the burning of incense? Is it the making of thyself of no estate?

²⁸Rather is it that ye *purpose!* For the try, the purpose of thine inner self, to *Him* is the righteousness. For He hath known all the vicissitudes of the earthly experience. He hath walked through the valley of the shadow of death. He hath seen the temptations of man from every phase that may come into thine own experience; and, yea, He hath given thee, "If ye will love me, believing I am able, I will deliver thee from that which so easily besets thee at *any* experience."

²⁹And it is thus that He stands; not as a Lord but as thy Brother, as thy Savior; that ye may know indeed the truth that gentleness, kindness, patience, brotherly love, beget—in thy heart of hearts, with Him—that peace, that harmony. Not as the world knoweth peace but as He gave: "That peace I give you; that ye may know that thy spirit, yea thy soul, beareth witness with me that ye are

mine—I am thine," even as the Father, the Son, the Holy Spirit.

[30]Even so may thy soul, thy mind, thy body, become aware of that which renews the hope, the faith, the patience within thee.

[31]And until ye show forth in His love that patience, ye cannot become aware of thy relationship with Him. Even as He has given, in patience ye become aware of being that soul—that seeketh the Father's house that is within even thine own consciousness.

[32]How? How, then, may ye approach the throne?

[33]Turn thou within. As ye meditate, give forth in thine OWN words these thoughts:

[34]*"Father, God, maker of heaven and earth! I am Thine—Thou art mine! As I claim that kinship with that holy love, keep Thou me in that consciousness of Thy presence abiding with me: that I may be that channel of blessings to others, that I may know Thy grace, Thy mercy, Thy love—even as I show such to my fellow man!"*

[35]And ye may be very sure the answer comes within.

[36]Thus, as ye apply—the answer comes. Not—by applying—do we mean a separation from the world. For even as He, ye are *in* the world but not *of* the world. But putting away the worldly things ye take hold upon the spiritual things, knowing that the worldly are but the shadows of the real.

[37]And thus, as ye come into the light of His countenance, it maketh thy heart glad in the consciousness of *"I am Thine—Thou art Mine."*

[38]Ready for questions.

[39](Q) What was the exact time of my physical birth?

(A) Eight-twenty in the morning.

[40](Q) What was the exact time of my soul birth?

(A) Only a few breaths after the physical birth. For as has been indicated to the soul, in the experiences in the earth—how beautiful have been thy joys, yea even thy sorrows, that they have kept alive that longing for a closer communion, a closer walk with Him!

And as the soul came then with a purposefulness, that "I—even I—may be able to show forth His love among those I meet day by day," there was no tarrying. For ye are learning, ye have gained, ye may apply, *"As ye sow, so shall ye reap."*

For God is not mocked. Though man may separate himself, it is against the purposes, the will of the love of truth. And only self may separate thee from the love of the Father. For He longeth, even as thy soul crieth out in the mornings, "Holy—holy art Thou, O Lord!"

[41](Q) If possible, what can I do to finish my earth's experience in this life?

(A) It is ever possible. Studying to show forth the Lord's death till He come again!!

What meaneth this?

Just living those that are the fruits of the spirit; namely: peace, harmony, long-suffering, brotherly love, patience. *These,* if ye show them forth in thy life, in thy dealings with thy fellow man, grow to be what? *Truth!* In Truth ye are *free,* from what? *Earthly* toil, *earthly* cares!

These then are not just axioms, not just sayings, but *living* truths!

Ye *are* happy in His *love! Hold* fast to that!

[42](Q) What is holding back my spiritual development?

(A) Nothing holding back—as has just been given—but *self.* For know, as has been given of old, "Though I take the wings of the morning in thought and fly unto the uttermost parts of the earth, Thou art there! Though I fly into the heavenly hosts, Thou art there! Though I make my bed in hell, Thou art there!"

And as He has promised, "When ye cry unto me, I *will* hear—and answer speedily."

Nothing prevents—only self. Keep self and the shadow away. Turn thy face to the light and the shadows fall behind.

43(Q) Please explain the meaning of a light I saw on the night of June 13th-14th, and a figure that appeared in the light.

(A) These are but the beginnings of that which may be thy experience. This followed a deep meditation, though much broke in between. But it is the fruit of not thought, but purpose, desire. For it has not entered the heart of man all the glories that have been prepared, nor all the beauties that may be experienced by those that seek His face.

These are but the signs, yea the *assurances,* that His presence abideth with thee.

Know He hath promised that if ye ask, ye shall receive. Be satisfied only then with the consciousness of His presence. Who? That in Whom ye have believed—that abides with thee. For "If ye will knock, I will open—for I stand at the door and knock."

If ye will but open thy tabernacle of consciousness to allow the holy to come in and sup with thee, yea *all* the beauties of peace and harmony *are* thine; for they are the birthright of each soul. For the soul is the portion of the Maker that makes thee individual, yet with the consciousness of being one with *God,* the *universe,* the *love*—that which *is* beauty and harmony.

44(Q) What is the meaning of the white lightning I have seen?

(A) That awakening that is coming. More and more as the white light comes to thee, more and more will there be the awakening. For as the lights are in the colors: In the green, healing; in the blue, trust; in the purple, strength; in the white, the light of the throne of mercy itself. Ye may never see these save ye have withheld judgment or shown mercy.

45(Q) What is my worst fault?

(A) What is ever the worst fault of each soul? *Self—self!* What is the meaning of self?

That the hurts, the hindrances are hurts to the self-consciousness; and these create what? Disturbing forces, and these bring about confusions and faults of every nature.

For the only sin of man is *selfishness!*

[46](Q) How may it be overcome?

(A) Just as has been given; showing mercy, showing grace, showing peace, long-suffering, brotherly love, kindness—even under the most *trying* circumstances.

For what is the gain if ye love those *only* that love thee? But to bring hope, to bring cheer, to bring joy, yea to bring a smile again to those whose face and heart are bathed in tears and in woe, is but making that divine love shine—shine—in thy own soul!

Then *smile,* be joyous, be glad! For the day of the Lord is at hand.

Who is thy Lord? Who is thy God?

Self? Or Him in Whom ye live and move and have thy being—that is *all* in All, God the Father, the Love—the *great* Hope, the Great Patience?

These are thy *all.*

Keep in the way that is arising before thee, more and more. And as ye open thy consciousness to the Great Consciousness within, there will arise more and more the white light.

For He is the light, and the life—eternal.

[47]We are through for the present.

Chapter 9

HOLISTIC HEALING

READING 1189-2

Fatigue, frequent emotional upset, loss of interest in life—these are common complaints in today's society. In fact, chronic fatigue syndrome is one of the most mystifying ailments of our times. Are these symptoms caused totally or in part by an undetected virus? Or might the origins of this dysfunction be more complex?

This case from the Cayce readings provides an interesting slant on a condition that was already known more than fifty years ago, although it may not have received the publicity it does now. This twenty-four-year-old woman sought clairvoyant advice from Edgar Cayce for a set of symptoms that sound all too familiar in the modern world. She was dispirited and had lost a sense of drive and ambition. Melancholic and drained of creative energy, she bordered on a nervous breakdown. Apparently there were also several unnamed physical complaints that were part of her problem.

As we might expect, the source of the Cayce material diagnosed the situation from a holistic (combining the physical, mental, and spiritual aspects of an individual) perspective and recommended a balanced set of steps to effect a healing.

Of special interest is the picture of what was causing her difficulties. She was a person of high ideals, but somehow a profound disappointment troubled her soul. Other people had failed to measure up to those high ideals; and because of her sensitivity, an inner rebellion was stimulated. That inward outrage and revolt created imbalances within her body, and hence her ailments.

It's a paradox of the human condition that high ideals can make us vulnerable. When we expect a lot—from ourselves or someone else—we increase the likelihood that conditions are going to fall short. The flavor of this irony is found in a number of other proverbs and adages. "Of him to whom much is given, much is expected." Or, from Jungian psychology, "The brighter the light, the darker the shadows." All these versions echo a common, paradoxical theme. The closer we come to the Ultimate, the more severe is the test or the level of our vulnerability.

How, then, did this reading counsel her to work for her own healing? How might he have advised any of us today who suffer from dispiritedness and fatigue? The first step requires attention to ideals. Get clear about values. Know what your ideal really is, making sure it's rooted in something beyond materialism. Anchor yourself in the reality of the invisible—in that which is timeless.

Next, recognize that disappointment can easily be a case of psychological projection. You may be disillusioned by the deeds of other people, but the paralyzing impact of that disenchantment suggests something else going on beneath the surface. No doubt you have some very good reasons for feeling let down by what someone said or did. But that failure has such a devastating impression, Cayce suggests, because "you have been disappointing." You have somehow disconnected from your own ideals—perhaps in that relationship, but just as likely in some other situation.

In the case of this young woman, the reading is very specific about how this loss of solidarity with her ideal has happened. The same process may or may not be exactly the way it happens for us. Apparently, she was inclined to "accede to wishes or desires of others, [in order] to hold or keep their respect . . . " The central point of direction in her life—what psychology would call one's *locus of control*—resided outside of her. This very misplacement led to disappointment (perhaps unconscious) with herself, which in turn made her much more likely to become disappointed in others—even to the point of becoming melancholic and dispirited. The chain reaction continued: loss of drive, fatigue, on the verge of a breakdown.

The reading holds out great hope for turning this condition around. It requires working at several levels concurrently. The first aspect is to get in touch with the *living* quality of one's ideal. The reading emphasizes this notion of vibrancy, activity, and a sense of being alive: "a *living* God, a *living* hope, a *living* faith—an *activative* experience!" Disappointment, despair, and depression are all linked to a general sluggishness of spirit. What's needed is movement and purposeful activity.

A second aspect of the recommended treatment involves physical procedures to stimulate well-being. For this individual and her condition, drugless approaches were emphasized. Someone today who has similar symptoms might choose to include medication prescribed by one's physician—especially if the psychological and spiritual elements can also be included. But in this instance, Cayce proposed hydrotherapy and "electrical" therapy. The latter apparently refers to one of the novel nontraditional low-voltage devices described in many other readings, and certainly does *not* refer to harsh electroshock treatment.

A third aspect to the program requires the use of free

will to create some disciplined, balanced rhythms to the day: " . . . let the body make out a schedule for itself . . . " So much time each day was to be spent improving attitudes about her relationship to God. A predetermined investment of time daily was to be devoted to physical exercise *and* relaxation. And a definite amount of time each day was to be focused on improving interpersonal relations. Anyone willing to make some choices and create a plan such as this—and then put it into application—is bound to see some healing results. And no doubt a big part of what's therapeutic in this approach is the enhanced sense of having some control over one's life.

Overall we can appreciate this particular Cayce reading, not only because it deals with a common, contemporary issue, but also because it's such a fine example of the holistic approach to healing. So much of what goes by the label "holistic" is really just a collection of nontraditional remedies. But here we see an insightful, coherent set of recommended treatment procedures that truly deal with body, mind, and spirit.

THE READING

This psychic reading, 1189-2, was given by Edgar Cayce on June 7, 1938. The conductor was Gertrude Cayce.

[1]EC: Yes, we have the body, [1189].

[2]Now as we find, in considering the particular disturbances which exist with this body—and these with the view of bringing normalcy and a revivifying of purposes, desires or ambitions—the body *whole* must be taken into consideration; that is, the physical, the mental, and the spiritual attributes of the body.

[3]For while each of the phases of a body-development is met within its own environ or phase, there are experi-

ences which arise within a body—as we find within this body—when all of these must be considered as they coordinate or cooperate one with another.

⁴And as is then to be understood, these *must* coordinate and cooperate—body, mind, soul—if there is to be the best reaction in the physical, mental or spiritual.

⁵Hence the injunction—from the spiritual aspects, and O that every soul would gain the concept, know and be conscious within—that "The Lord Thy God Is *One!*"

⁶Now with this body we find there has been an exceeding upset in the ideals of the body-mind; coming from disappointments in individuals and in the reaction to that which is the ideal of the entity within itself.

⁷And being of a supersensitive nature, it has (the mental) *rebelled* at these conditions.

⁸Now the expressions of these reactions are within the *physical* forces of the body.

⁹Hence we have been gradually on the border of a nervous breakdown, as it would be called by most pathologists or psychologists.

¹⁰Yet through the emotions these have produced, as we find, *definite* reactions in the physical forces of the body; as related to the nervous system, both cerebrospinal and sympathetic. And those areas that find greater distress are where the cerebrospinal and the sympathetic or imaginative centers coordinate with the physical reactions of the body.

¹¹Hence we have had periods of uncontrollable melancholy. We have had periods of the uncontrollable overflow of the ducts that express emotions; inability of perfect assimilation—which immediately upsets the metabolism of the whole physical body.

¹²These then, as we find, are both pathological and psychological conditions that disturb the equilibrium of the body.

¹³These are not as faults, these are not as conditions

that may not be corrected; yet—from the very nature of their affectation through the emotions—both the physical *and* the mental are to be taken into consideration in giving counsel or advice for corrective forces for this body.

[14]First:

[15]*Who* is to say as to what must be any individual's ideal? But know, O Soul, that it must be founded in spiritual, unseen, everlasting things!

[16]What are these?

[17]Faith, hope, love; without thought of self.

[18]For when self or the own ego becomes disappointed, know that you have been disappointing *in* your relationships to that which produces or may produce same.

[19]Not that it is always necessary to accede to wishes or desires of others, to hold or keep their respect, love, hope or faith. But know in *whom* as well as in what you believe! And if thy faith is founded in the spiritual, the Creative, the constructive forces, it brings peace and harmony.

[20]Then let thy heart, thy mind, determine within itself.

[21]See and be in that attitude as given of old; letting others do as they will or may, but for thee ye will cleave to a *living* God, a *living* hope, a *living* faith—an *activative* experience!

[22]Thus, as ye do this, the other things may pass.

[23]As you find, there has been created an inactivative force—other than repellent—between the sympathetic nervous system and the judgments; or the cerebrospinal nerve reaction of positive fact or nature.

[24]Hence as we will find, change of scene and of environment will be well.

[25]But *first* we would have the low electrical forces that would *attune* the bodily forces to coordinate one with another.

[26]Then also we would have the hydrotherapy and the electrical forces.

²⁷*Do not* resort to drug of *any* nature. For upon same as to bring those appetites that would become—the vibrations of the mental and spiritual will only rebel, or so feed upon same as to bring those appetites that would become—to the mental and spiritual forces of the entity—repellent in their end.

²⁸Work and associate with those influences or forces wherein there is help being lent or given to others. This will also create an atmosphere, an attitude for the body mentally and physically that will be constructive.

²⁹For the very nature of the entity, and of the impelling influences that we have indicated for the body, is to be *busy!*

³⁰Then let it be in *constructive* forces, but keep busy—no matter in what direction, keep busy!

³¹As we find, these adhered to will bring about the better reactions.

³²At first it may appear that these are not very definite, but let the body make out a schedule for itself in this manner:

³³"So much time each day *(and do it!)* I will give to the improvement of my mental concept of my relationships to Creative Forces of God.

³⁴"So much time each day I will give to *physical* relaxation and exertion for expression, for the activities to produce the proper coordinant relationships between mind and the body.

³⁵"So much time I will give *(and give it!)*, each day, to putting into *practice* that which is *perceived* and *conceived*," as to thy relationships to the Creative Forces, thy relationships to thy fellow man.

³⁶And not necessarily those in high places, nor altogether those who have lost hope. For the body, mind and soul needs the encouragements as well as the concrete forces of example where hope has been and is lost, that must be revived by thy activity.

[37]Keep in the open oft, and in thy activity.

[38]And we will find—before the season has gone—a new outlook upon the experiences in this life!

[39]Ready for questions.

[40](Q) How should the low electrical forces be used?

(A) Those of the direct current; as in the low galvanic or the low violet, or the like.

[41](Q) How often would you suggest the hydrotherapy treatments?

(A) Once or twice a week in the beginning, and then gradually farther apart.

Do these things as we have indicated, and as we find we will bring that as described.

[42](Q) Who would you recommend to follow these suggested treatments?

(A) Choose this for yourself.

[43](Q) How may I best overcome the spells of emotional hysteria which interfere so seriously with my work?

(A) As indicated. *Doing* something! but considering body, mind *and* purpose of soul!

[44](Q) How may I overcome constant fatigue physically which results in disinterestedness in people and in my work?

(A) As indicated; in the manners that have been outlined.

[45](Q) How may I regain my former drive and ambitions?

(A) Just as has been given. There must be reestablished, as it were, the *ideal;* and things that have made the body and mind, and the very physical forces afraid, must be wiped away as a tear.

[46]We are through for the present.

Chapter 10

COORDINATING BODY SYSTEMS

READING 1120-2

Most A.R.E. members probably have never read a Cayce health reading in its entirety. Our knowledge of Cayce's pioneering, holistic vision of the human body is based on pertinent excerpts and on books written *about* the material by experts. But there's much to be gained from seeing the total approach Cayce took in his physical readings. It's worth the effort to carefully study a complete health reading.

Of course, each physical reading was geared to the particular needs of the recipient. Each focused on a very specific malady and recommended treatment procedures that would agree with the idiosyncrasies of that person. But in spite of the fact that each health reading was "customized," reading 1120-2 is one that contains useful information for nearly all of us. It's a fine example of Cayce-the-health-advisor at his best. This reading has universal value—in part because the twenty-nine-year-old man's symptoms resemble ones that so many people have in today's stressful world. What's more, it demonstrates so clearly Cayce's model for how the body works.

Some months earlier this man had received a life reading; now he was requesting health advice because of chronic fatigue and periodic headaches. (See paragraph 17 for Cayce's clairvoyant view of the symptoms—all of which he traces back to a root problem with imbalances at the second and third dorsal vertebrae, just a few inches below the base of the neck.) Getting a health reading from a psychic was, no doubt, an unconventional and controversial move for this man to take. In paragraph 9, Cayce even warns that the theories in this reading will likely be disputed (presumably by Mr. [1120]'s traditionalist doctor).

The reading begins with a rather positive picture. In paragraph 2 we find Cayce's overall analysis: this man is in generally good health. However, the bothersome little disturbances are symptomatic of conditions that, left uncorrected, could later develop into much more serious problems.

In the very structure of what follows in this reading, we find a key element in the Cayce model of how the body works. He outlines the status of three principal systems:

• The circulatory (or "blood supply"). When the circulation of the blood is hindered, it affects the capacity to assimilate both nutrients and oxygen. What's more, that same circulatory system (including the lymph system) must be working effectively for the body to be able to properly get rid of waste products. (Cayce often used the word "emunctory" which means waste removal.)

• The nervous (or the "nerve forces"). This includes two primary sub-systems. First is the cerebrospinal, which includes large portions of the brain, the spinal cord, and nerves which connect to the spinal cord and make possible both sensory awareness and voluntary control over the muscles. Second is the autonomic nervous system, which has control centers in the brain and yet operates generally outside of one's conscious awareness. The autonomic system, in turn, has two parts: the sympathetic (which largely relates to the activation of internal organs) and the parasympathetic (which is more concerned with quieting and regenerative processes in the body).

In the physical readings Cayce was especially concerned with the junction points at which the cerebrospinal and sympathetic interact—ganglia located alongside the vertebrae of the spinal column. When there is misalignment or subluxation of the vertebrae, it can cause an imbalanced relationship between these two nerve systems, resulting in a wide variety of problems for the internal organs. (This reading gives a succinct primer on the topic in paragraphs 8-13. It shows why Cayce so often recommended osteopathic or chiropractic adjustments.)

• The array of internal organs. Cayce usually hones in on just a few organs that are especially related to the disturbance. Surprisingly in some health readings, the organs mentioned often include ones that seemingly have nothing to do with the problem since no pain or discomfort has been experienced there.

It's not easy reading to get through the diagnosis of these three systems. But don't get dismayed if you fail to understand entirely what Cayce is saying. Instead, look for the central patterns and the key themes. One is certainly the *interconnectedness* of the body systems. This theory is becoming more widely accepted in medical science today. A longstanding tradition in medicine has assumed that the body's systems tend to operate more independently of each other than Cayce's theory supposes. But one example of a changing attitude is the new field of psychoneuroimmunology, which has begun to demonstrate that the mind, nervous system, and immune system are directly linked.

Another key theme in Cayce's health model is that *many ailments are a "reflex"*—that is, a disturbing but quite natural reaction to something that's out of balance somewhere else in the body. Notice, for example, how paragraphs 24 and 25 describe Mr. [1120]'s digestive problems as a reflex rather than a problem directly with those organs themselves.

Even if we aren't experiencing the exact symptoms of Mr. [1120], there is solid advice in this reading about maintaining overall balance and coordination in order to promote health. Furthermore, through this one sample reading, we get an especially clear image of how Cayce understood the body, and we see the type of strategy he often used in designing a set of treatment procedures for healing.

Finally, here's an interesting postscript: Five weeks after the reading, Mr. [1120] wrote to Cayce: "I am following out the treatments that you outlined in my reading and find that they have helped considerably."

THE READING

This psychic reading, 1120-2, was given by Edgar Cayce on April 17, 1936. The conductor was Gertrude Cayce.

¹EC: Yes, we have the body here, [1120], present in this room.

²Now, as we find, the general physical forces of the body in many ways appear to be well. And the reactions in most of same are good. Yet we find there are hindrances, disturbances and impulses the correction of which now would not only be a helpfulness to those conditions that disturb the body at times in a greater degree than is shown in the immediate, but would assist in preventing disturbances that would be of a much more violent nature to deal with—if allowed to become more and more a condition to be reckoned with by a perfectly normal functioning body.

³These have to do, as we find, with impingements that

exist in the nervous system, as will be seen by their effect upon the body as well as in the disturbances or nature of same as produced.

⁴Then, these are the conditions as we find them with this body, [1120] we are speaking of:

⁵First, *in the blood supply,* from the disturbed condition in the nervous system (that is, the cerebrospinal impulse), (more than the sympathetic) there are hindrances with the *manners* of assimilation. Thus there are those tendencies for a slowing of the circulation in its return from the extremities, or through the arteries into the veins.

⁶Hence we have in the metabolism of the system an unbalancing, but with the corrections of that which has produced same in the first there would be a more helpful condition in creating a normal equilibrium.

⁷*In the nerve forces themselves of the body,* we find: As has been indicated, here is the basis or the cause of the disturbances.

⁸In some time back there was a hindrance in the ganglia of the 2nd and 3rd dorsal, that has produced there the tendency for a lack of proper incentive for its coordination with the vegetative or sympathetic nerve system as *well* as an excess of activity in the deeper nerves as from the junction there of the cerebrospinal and sympathetic with the organs of assimilation.

⁹Let it be understood, then, by the body, the manner in which this disturbance arising there affects the system (for it will be disputed to the body):

¹⁰Each segment connects with a centralized area between the sympathetic and the cerebrospinal systems, or in the spinal cord impulse itself. In *specific* centers there runs a connecting link between the segments. And such an one exists in this particular center as we have indicated.

¹¹In each of those areas called a ganglion there is a

bursa, or a small portion of nerve tissue that acts as a regulator or a conductor, or as a director of impulses from the nerve forces to the organs of the body that are affected by this portion of the nervous system.

[12]Not that any one organ, any one functioning of an organ, receives all its impulse from one ganglion or one center along the spine; but that these slowing up by a deficiency in the activity because of pressure produce— as here—a lesion, or an attempt of the blood flow (that is, the lymph and emunctory flow) to shield any injured portion or any pressure. This ofttimes increases the amount of pressure to other portions of the body.

[13]Hence we have an incoordination with the activities in other portions of the body. But with the correction or removal of pressure from such an area, the affected portions will be relieved; that is, as in this body here, the effects to the sensory forces—as the throat, the nasal passages, the eyes, that are affected by this lack of the blood flow.

[14]For, remember, though the heart beats—it is governed, or the circulation is governed by nerve impulse that acts as a supervisor or an overseer would, in conducting to the activity of the system that which not only supplies the nutriment for its individual functioning but also the eliminations of drosses from such used activity, as well as supplying nutriment from that assimilated by the circulation in its entirety for the recuperation and rebuilding.

[15]And remember, these conditions are constantly going on in the system at all times.

[16]What, then, are the conditions produced by this subluxation, in this particular body?

[17]There are times, even with the full-blooded circulation or full quantity that exists, when the outer portions of the body (that is, through the superficial circulation) become as deadened for a period; a few moments is suf-

ficient to make for pallidness to the body; easily tired by walking of any great amount; easily tired at times—or even more so—(than by walking at certain periods) by sitting around; or worrying about or being overanxious about conditions brings headaches, fullness in the throat, upsetting at times of the digestive forces and the reactions to the whole of the assimilating system, as *well* as producing for the general forces of the body a tendency towards acidity throughout the system. So, the eliminations even through the alimentary canal become involved.

[18]Now, in taking those things that assist in producing a stimulation to either the eliminations or to cause a balance in the acidity and alkalinity of the body, or so that we make for an increased flow or a draining of conditions through the lymph flow through the head or soft tissue of throat and head, the condition is allayed. But the *causes* of these effects, the causes of those things that upset the digestive forces, the causes of that which has made for a disturbance through the eye, the ear, nose, throat, in their relative relation one to another, arise from those areas indicated—as we find.

[19]*In the functioning of the organs themselves:*

[20]As to the brain forces, when there is a *physical* coordination as related to their activity with the system, we find that—as we have indicated for the body through its *mental* development—the body's mental abilities and associations are able to segregate, able to make for definite impressions upon activities in given directions. But if these are hindered by the tiring that comes on, or those disturbances through the organs' functioning as indicated, these naturally will become *laggard*—or the abilities of the body will become hindered.

[21]In the throat, bronchi, lungs and larynx—as we have indicated—there occurs at times, as a tendency from this improper pulsation, and especially from the specific

ganglia referred to, the more susceptibility of the body to congestions through such areas; though organically these are very good.

[22]Heart's activity is as we have indicated.

[23]Digestive forces again are disturbed or upset at times, nervously; but organically, as for their balance, as a coordinant tendency through the system, very good. And when such corrections are made, we would find these disturbing reactions would be overcome.

[24]As to the activity of the spleen, the pancreas, the liver, the gall duct area: When foods are assimilated, these organs function for or in producing the juices or fluids that act upon elements in the foods that are assimilated in an acid and alkaline content from the stomach itself. With these hindrances, there becomes at times the tendency for these to become acid.

[25]Hence through the alimentary canal disturbances arise at times; but these are reflex, as we find, as may be indicated, rather than being organic or even functional in these portions of the system.

[26]*Then, in meeting the needs of these conditions,* as we find:

[27]First we would begin with the use of the hydrotherapy activity that would not only give periods for specific exercise but *at* such periods have a massage and an adjustment in those *particular* areas indicated; that is, the upper dorsal, specifically in the 3rd and 2nd, coordinant with the cervical area, to the base of the brain.

[28]Also we would add with same an electrical vibration as a portion of such treatments.

[29]And we will find the bodily functionings, the muscular forces, the whole general outlook, will be brought to a normal force in this body, [1120].

[30]Ready for questions.

[31](Q) What type of electrical treatment should be given?

(A) Either the violet ray or the *alternating* current of a

sinusoidal vibration that is *hand* applied.

[32](Q) Should these adjustments be made osteopathically or chiropractically, or just how?

(A) As indicated, in the proper regulated hydrotherapist treatment we have the masseurs that would make such an adjustment when these are taken.

Use these as at intervals; once a week, or twice a week one week, once a week the next week, twice a week the next week, then once a week; and then whenever there are those tendencies for the tiredness or sluggishness through the activity of the liver or the eliminations, or pains to the head or even a heaviness there.

And, as we find, we will keep the body fit.

[33](Q) These treatments will relieve the tiredness?

(A) This, as we have indicated, is what these are for! When we remove those pressures that cause these conditions, then we remove that feeling, see?

[34](Q) What treatment should be used for the scalp?

(A) The electrical treatment with the violet ray for this particular body, we find, would be the *most* beneficial.

[35](Q) Will this prevent the hair falling out?

(A) As indicated, there have been those tendencies for the superficial and the deeper circulations to be disturbed. They are breaking away, they are not coordinating. A stimulation to any portion of the body for greater activity, by not too much but as using the comb of such a hand violet ray machine through the hair and head, will make for such stimulation as to make more growth of the hair and also a better growth of the hair.

[36](Q) What about general exercise, golf and tennis?

(A) Well, he'll find his golf stroke will improve a great deal if he will remove this pressure between the shoulders as indicated!

These, to be sure (the exercise), are helpful conditions. Do these.

[37]We are through for the present.

Chapter 11

PHYSICAL FITNESS

READING 341-31

This health reading, one of Cayce's best, contains the universal principles of good health.

Balance is a central theme. The concept of balance sounds simple enough: keep an equilibrium in your lifestyle so that no part of you gets short-changed. A superficial understanding of balance might tempt you to compartmentalize your life neatly into time periods that allow you to give attention one-by-one to each aspect of yourself. But this reading goes deeper and shows how the physical body, mental body, and spiritual body interrelate. Their mutual dependency is the essence of Cayce's approach to health.

In fact, this reading seems to emphasize not compartmentalizing life, but instead discovering how the many aspects of life are knit together. For example, consider the admonition, "Know how to apply the rules of *metaphysical* operations to a corncob . . . " There's really only one universe—not a metaphysical realm separate from a material one. What works in one dimension should work in the others as well. The rules that govern the world of the mind have their counterpart in the physical body. In other words, what works at a grand level of scale should work at the smallest level the same way. As the reading put it, "each cell . . . each corpuscle, is a whole *universe* in itself." We can even look for the way human anatomy may symbolically depict a psychological truth— blood passes through the liver twice for every one time through the heart, just as we should "think twice before [we] speak once . . . "

Authentic balance, then, requires sensitivity to inter-relationship—not merely a check-off list of all the good activities one ought to squeeze into a single day. Unfortunately, that's how some people try to achieve balance; and yet in their hectic efforts to get it all done, they sometimes undermine their own health. And so, we should add to the concept of balance that of relation-ship.

The story of what happens to food as it's eaten and digested is a beautiful illustration of Cayce's philosophy of health. Physical conditions beyond the organs of di-gestion play a important role. This man was instructed to make sure both his mental and physical bodies were suf-ficiently tired by the end of the day so that his body would even be able to respond properly to his diet.

Later, he was encouraged to try a visualization exer-cise as he ate—"That thou eatest, *see* it *doing* that *thou* would *have* it do"—a clear illustration of mind-body in-teraction. In fact, this simple exercise is one of the best ways to test Cayce's approach to "health through bal-ance." And yet, in a home research project, "Three-Step Body Tune-Up," A.R.E. members found this discipline to be particularly difficult to complete (or, more often, to remember) because of our hurried eating habits.

Even more dramatic, though, is the reference to the pla-cebo effect—"Give one a dose of clear *water*, with the im-pression that it will act as salts . . . " Cayce was ahead of his times in pointing out just how significant this phe-nomenon really is. The impact of belief and expectation upon the physical body is a vivid illustration of the body-mind connection.

Cayce made reference to the biblical account of Daniel, demonstrating how the food we consume stimulates particular states of consciousness. By self-observation we may have already seen hints of this relationship between body and mind. Here's an area that is ripe for research. In fact, some preliminary findings regarding nutrition and mental illness suggest that certain culprit foods (such as sugar and white bread) may aggravate mental disorders.

What also makes this reading special is the spiritual component. Many medical researchers today recognize the mind-body relationship. But this reading clearly suggests that "health through balance" must include the spiritual body, too. That means having a purpose in life; that means appreciating our physical bodies as gifts of God, the vehicles through which we can serve the divine plan. Engaging the spiritual body in an authentically balanced lifestyle also implies consciously looking for the living spirit, expecting to see God in the midst of material life—"in the wind, the sun, the earth, the flowers, the inhabitant *of* the earth . . . "

Surely the Cayce principles are right on the cutting edge of today's health philosophy. As encouraging as new developments in holistic and mind-body research may be, this reading calls us to an even bigger vision.

THE READING

This psychic reading, 341-31, was given by Edgar Cayce on March 10, 1931. The conductor was Gertrude Cayce.

[The first few paragraphs contained specific physical advice rather than general guidelines.]

6EC: . . . It would be well for the body to so conduct, so

arrange the activities of the body as to be better *balanced* as to the mental and the physical attributes of the body. Take more outdoor exercise, that—that brings into play the muscular forces of the body. It isn't that the mental should be numbed, or should be cut off from their operations or their activities—but make for a more evenly, more perfectly balanced body-physical *and* mental. Know how to apply the rules of *metaphysical* operations to a corncob, or to a fence rail, or to a hammer, an axe, a walking cane, as well as the *theories* of this, that, or other mind, that in nine cases in ten is seen to become a storehouse for mental deficiencies of *physical* energies! Now get the difference! It is not mental unbalance, but a mental body may be so *overused* as to allow physical energies to become *detrimental* forces *in a physical body;* for each energy *must* expend itself in *some* direction, even as a thought that takes form brings in to being a mental image. Is that image in the position of being a *building* force cooperative with the energies of the physical body? Or do they *destroy* some motive force in the physical without allowing an outlet for its activity?

⁷Then, be a well-*rounded* body. Take specific, *definite* exercises morning and evening. Make the body *physically,* as well as mentally, tired and those things that have been producing those conditions where sleep, inertia, poisons in system from non-eliminations, will disappear—and so will the body respond to the diets.

⁸Now, in the matter of diets—*one* activity is necessary, if there is to be a mental diet—or if there is to be a diet for a well-rounded *physically* useful, *mentally* useful, *spiritually* useful body. But there is the lack of vitamins as B and C, in this body. One, the C, stamina for mental energies that are carried in the white tissue in nerve energy and plexus. B, as is of calcium, of silicon, of iron. These would be well-balanced, will those of the food values that carry same be taken, but *unless* the activities

physical for the body are such as to put same into *activity* they become drosses and set *themselves* to become operative, irrespective of *other* conditions. (This as aside, but as very well in keeping with the circumstances or conditions.) Vitamins in a body are elements that are combative with, or in opposition to, the various activities of a living organism, and may be termed—and well termed—as those of bacilli of any nature within a human or physical organism. That's what we are talking of, or dealing with in this body.

⁹Now, when these are taken into the system, if they are *not* put to work by the *activities* of the *system*—either physical or mental—they become *destructive* tissue, for they *affect* the plasm [plasma] of the blood supply or the emunctory and lymph which is another name for a portion of a blood supply in a system.

¹⁰Then, in the meeting of the diet—be sure the activities, physically, and mentally, are in keeping with; and *do not do* these *spasmodically,* but *be* consistent—for the physical body, the mental body, the spiritual body, is as "Grow in grace, in knowledge, in understanding."

¹¹That thou eatest, *see* it *doing* that *thou* would *have* it do. Now there is often considered as to why do those of either the vegetable, mineral, or combination compounds, have different effects under different conditions? It is the *consciousness* of the *individual body!* Give one a dose of clear *water,* with the impression that it will act as salts—how often will it act in that manner?

¹²Just as the impressions to the whole of the organism, for each cell of the bloodstream, each corpuscle, is a whole *universe* in itself. Do not eat like a canary and expect to do *manual* labor. Do not eat like a rail splitter and expect to do the work of a mind reader or a university professor, but be *consistent* with those things that make for—even as the *universe* is builded. In the layers of one is dependent upon the activity of another. One

that fills the mind, the very being, with an expectancy of God will see His movement, His manifestation, in the wind, the sun, the earth, the flowers, the inhabitant *of* the earth; and so as is builded in the body, is it to gratify *just* an appetite, or is it taken to fulfill an office that *will* the better make, the better magnify, that the body, the mind, the soul, *has* chosen to stand *for?* and it will not matter so much what, where, or *when*—but knowing *that* it is consistent with that—that is desired to be accomplished *through* that body!

[13]As has been given of old, when the children of Israel stood with the sons of the heathen and all ate from the king's table, that which was taken that only exercised the imagination of the body in physical desires—as strong drink, strong meats, condiments that magnify desires within the body—this builded as Daniel well understood, not for *God's* service—but he chose rather that the *everyday*, the common things would be given, that the bodies, the minds, might be a more perfect channel for the manifestations of *God;* for the forces of the Creator are in *every* force that is made manifest *in* the earth.

[14]Few are able, even as the prophet of old, to see God in battle, in the shedding of blood, in the thunder, in the lightning, in the earthquake, in the various tumults in nature—but *all* may experience Him in the still small voice within! Do *thou* likewise, and the body is the temple *of* the living God, and is a *reasonable* service that we present same holy and acceptable unto Him.

[15]Just as great a sin to *over* eat as to over drink; to over *think* as to over act! *In* that thou buildest, do even as He. Make thine body, thine *mind,* ready for *every* occasion that arises in the life. Think well on what was given, "*Why* could not *we* cast him out? Such is done only—*only*—through fasting and prayer." When thou prayest, enter into thine closet—that is, within self—not shutting oneself away from the world, but closing self to God's *pres-*

ence, and pray in secret and the reward will be in the open; for, as was given, "Men do not light a candle and put it under a bushel, but it is set—*set*—on a hill, that it may give *life,* light, unto all."

[16]So, in conducting thine own life—make the physical corrections necessary, yes—but make also thy mind and thine body, thine going in and thine coming out, thine activities day by day, consistent *with*—and the reward will be—an exemplary life, a *goodly* body, an *open* mind, a *loving* spirit!

[17]Few may show forth that even felt in the heart with the liver bad, for twice does the blood pass through the liver to once in the heart. The liver is the clearinghouse both for that of the blood in and out of the heart and lungs. So in the conduct of the life, in the study, think twice before you speak once—for there's only *one* tongue but two eyes. There is only *one* heart but seven lobes in the liver; and in thine hands—use that thou hast, and thine eye will be *single* in service, thine tongue will be loosed in the right direction.

Chapter 12

JESUS THE CHRIST

READING 5749-4

No Cayce reading is any clearer than this one about the fact that each of us can have a direct and personal relationship with Christ. That message was delivered on a summer afternoon over sixty years ago to some of the members of the original "A Search for God" group. Three of those present had brought their own experiences, hoping for an interpretation. They wondered whether what had seemed to be communication with Christ was actually that.

From the moment Cayce began the opening discourse, it was clear that this was to be a remarkable reading. In well over 99 percent of the other readings, Cayce's own superconscious mind offers the information. But reading 5749-4 seems to be one of those rare instances in which he "channels" the consciousness of some other being—in this case, the apostle John. There is a certain ambiguity about how much of this reading is given by John and how much is from Cayce's own higher self. But in at least three places, John specifically announces himself.

But what makes this reading so special is not so much the unexpected communication from John. It is the promise which is offered. Anyone who sincerely desires a direct contact with Christ—*and* acts in a way to reflect that desire—can expect an experience.

Where is Christ anyway? Where is He to be found? This reading speaks directly to those questions. Yes, it's natural for the physical, conscious mind to think in terms of time and space. Those are the familiar categories that help us understand things. But it may get frustrating if we try to pin Christ down to a location so that we can go there and make a personal contact. He isn't in the earth plane in a body, in the familiar sense. Instead, Cayce suggests here that if we insist on linking the Christ presence to a particular spatial location, then we should understand Him to be "in the individual entity." That is to say, He's found within us, and it is a relationship that becomes conscious through attunement.

Attunement is the essential quality that makes such a personal relationship possible. The Christ Consciousness is a level of universal awareness that resides in every soul. And it is *also* the consciousness of an extraordinary being who lived in the physical dimension twenty centuries ago and who still exists as a living presence—someone who is very much active in the spirit world.

How do we get in contact with Him? By a sort of resonance of vibration that is possible when we reach a state of wholeness—a condition in which we feel in sync with ourselves so that our desires and our talents are going in the same direction. Probably we've all had times in which we experienced that kind of wholeness, and perhaps in those moments we intuited just how connected we are with the invisible sphere.

The idea of attunement is central to many subjects in the Cayce readings, including meditation and healing.

Attunement involves the body, the mind, and the will—getting these factors in harmony with the spirit. Maybe it's tempting to leave out the bodily factor and believe that getting ourselves ready to contact Christ is purely a psychological matter. But as this reading points out, attunement gets right down to each atom of the physical body!

In the mental realm, there are at least two keys. First is faith. Knowing that Christ can and will communicate directly with us has a potent, attuning effect. The second key is the surrender of fear. As Christ initiates a personal relationship, it's often with the words, "Be not afraid." This may be necessary because something in us shies away from such an encounter. Fear—more than any other emotion—can interrupt attunement.

The third factor in attunement requires right use of will. Here's an element that's often ignored, but Cayce puts it right in the heart of his advice. If any of us wants a direct, personal relationship with Christ, then we've got to work actively to "[make] the will of self one with His will . . . " More than anything else that means letting our deeds reflect our beliefs and faith. It means putting into application what we hold in our hearts. The promise offered in this reading—actually just a reaffirmation of the biblical promise—is that Christ will come to anyone who wills it to be so and then "acts in love to make [it] possible."

Deep down inside, each of us knows just what that means. A part of us may protest (Oh, if only I knew for sure exactly what Christ wants me to be doing!). But in a quiet place of knowing—a place that often we don't like to admit is very familiar—we're really certain of what's required. We know that it has something to do with taking time to be present to other people and really hearing them out, rather than being caught up in the busy demands of our own agendas and lists of "things to be accomplished." We know that what's required has something to do with putting quality and excellence into all our efforts, especially those that affect other people. And just

as surely, in that quiet place of knowing, it has been revealed to us that we are quite *capable* of putting the
Christ Spirit first in our lives. What's asked of us is not
outrageous, it's not unreasonable, and it's "not grievous."
It's within our reach.

THE READING

*This psychic reading, 5749-4, was given by Edgar Cayce
on August 6, 1933. The conductor was Gertrude Cayce.*

[1]GC: You will have before you the Norfolk Study Group
#1, members of which are present in this room, who seek
more knowledge of, and that a reading be given on, Jesus
the Christ. We would appreciate all knowledge that
might be given on Him at this time, after which you will
answer the questions that may be asked by each individual present.

[2]EC: Yes, we have the group as gathered here; and their
work, their desires. We will seek that as may be given at
this time.

[3]"I, John, would speak with thee concerning the Lord,
the Master, as He walked among men. As given, if all that
He did and said were written, I suppose the world would
not contain all that may be said."

[4]As He, the Christ, is in His glory that was ordained of
the Father, He may be approached by those who in sincerity and earnestness seek to know Him—and to be
guided by Him. As He has given, by faith all things are
made possible through belief in His name.

[5]Believest thou? Then let thine activities bespeak that
thou wouldst have, in spirit, in truth.

[6]Seek, then, each in your own way and manner, to
magnify that you, as souls, as beings, would make manifest of His love, in the way He will show thee day by day.

[7]As He came into the world, as man knows the world,

then He became as man; yet in the spirit world He seeks to make manifest that sought by those who do His biddings.

[8]For, as He gave, "If ye love me, keep my commandments. These are not new, and are not grievous, that ye love one another—even as the Father loveth me."

[9](Q) [993]: Please explain why during meditation last Monday noon I had the longing to seek more knowledge of, and a reading on, Jesus the Christ.

(A) The inner self approached nearer the attunement of the consciousness of the Christ presence.

The Christ Consciousness is a universal consciousness of the Father Spirit. The Jesus consciousness is that man builds as body worship.

In the Christ Consciousness, then, there is the oneness of self, self's desires, self's abilities, made in atonement with the forces that may bring to pass that which is sought by an individual entity or soul. Hence at that particular period self was in accord. Hence the physical consciousness had the desire to make it an experience of the whole consciousness of self.

Seek this the more often. He will speak with thee, for His promises are true—every one of them.

[10](Q) [560]: Please explain: While meditating I had the realization of the forces within and the forces without being the one and the same force. Then as if someone said: "Why not look to the within?" When I turned to the within, I received a realization of the Christ which seemed to take form in body.

(A) In this the body-consciousness experienced much that "I, even John, experienced when I looked behind me from the cave and saw that the without and within are *one*," when the desires of the heart make each atom of the physical body vibrate with the consciousness of, the belief and the faith and the presence of, the Christ life, the Christ Consciousness.

Life is an essence of the Father. The Christ, taking up the life of the man Jesus, becomes life in glory; and may be glorified in each atom of a physical body that attunes self to the consciousness and the *will* of the Christ Spirit.

[11](Q) [69]: Is the Celestial Sphere a definite place in the universe or is it a state of mind?

(A) When an entity, a soul, passes into any sphere, with that it has builded in its celestial body, it must occupy—to a finite mind—space, place, time. Hence, to a finite mind, a body can only be in a place, a position. An attitude, sure—for that of a onement with, or attunement with, the Whole.

For, God is love; hence occupies a space, place, condition, and *is* the Force that permeates all activity.

So, Christ is the ruling force in the world that man, in his finite mind—the material body, must draw to self of that sphere of which the entity, the soul, is a part, of whatever period of experience, to be conscious of an existence in that particular sphere or plane.

[12](Q) Is Jesus the Christ on any particular sphere or is He manifesting on the earth plane in another body?

(A) As just given, all power in heaven, in earth, is given to Him who overcame. Hence He is of Himself in space, in the force that impels through faith, through belief, in the individual entity. As a Spirit Entity. Hence not in a body in the earth, but may come at will to him who *wills* to be one with, and acts in love to make same possible.

For, He shall come as ye have seen Him go, in the *body* He occupied in Galilee. The body that He formed, that was crucified on the cross, that rose from the tomb, that walked by the sea, that appeared to Simon, that appeared to Philip, that appeared to "I, even John."

[13](Q) Wherever He is, how may I contact Him so that I may see Him and hear Him speak?

(A) The making of the will of self one with His will makes a whole attunement with Him. He *will*, with the making of self in accord and desiring same, speak with thee. "Be not afraid, it is I."

[14](Q) [585]: Was the vision I saw early one morning several months ago a vision of the Master?

(A) A passing shadow, yes. Pray rather to the Son, the Father through the Son, that He walks with thee—and He *will* walk and talk with thee. Be *not* satisfied with *any* other. He may oft give His angels charge concerning thee, yet know the Master's touch, the Master's voice; for He may walk and talk with thee. *He* is the Way; there is no other. He in body suffered; for himself, yea—for thee also. Wilt thou turn, then, to any other?

[15](Q) When Jesus the Christ comes the second time, will He set up His kingdom on earth and will it be an everlasting kingdom?

(A) Read His promises in that ye have written of His words, even as "I gave." He shall rule for a thousand years. Then shall Satan be loosed again for a season.

[16](Q) [379]: How may I raise my vibrations so as to contact the Christ?

(A) Making the will, the desire of the heart, one with His, believing in faith, in patience, all becomes possible in Him, through Him to the Father; for He gave it as it is. Believest thou?

Then, "according to thy faith be it done in thee."

[17]We are through.

Chapter 13

EASTER

READING 5749-6

One cannot fully understand the philosophy and worldview of the Cayce readings without including their Christology. This Easter message was given to a small group of Cayce's key followers (many of whom he felt had previous lifetimes in the first century with Jesus). It contains one of the clearest and most succinct statements of just how pivotal a role the Christ played in human history.

But how does this message compare to the meaning of Easter which has been presented by others? If we think of Edgar Cayce as a modern theologian, exactly how would his message compare to other leading Christian thinkers?

At one end of a continuum are those who claim that the work of Jesus the Christ was all-encompassing. Anyone who merely makes a confession of faith in Jesus will have all of his or her sins and shortcomings done away with.

At the other extreme are those Christians who profoundly admire Jesus' life, but they see Him only as an example of the way we should live. His life, death, and resurrection did nothing directly for our own errant lives except to show us a better way.

Cayce's position seems to be somewhere near the

middle of this continuum. As we can clearly see in reading 5749-6, he asserts that Christ made (and still makes) an intervention that deeply alters the spiritual condition in which we find ourselves. However, Cayce's Christology would never go so far as to say that a mere confession of belief is enough. We each must learn to experience Christlike lives; we each must take responsibility for our shortcomings and walk that long pathway back to God.

From this centrist position, the readings can then say that in Jesus the Christ we have both (1) the power that redeems us and (2) the pattern that gives us an inspiring example about how to live daily.

Why then did the Christ come into the earth and take on a body of flesh? This ancient mystery of the incarnation has perplexed Christians for centuries. In trying to answer this question, everyone seems to agree that humanity had (and still has) a profound need for help. Where Cayce adds a crucial twist is his idea about redemption itself. The goal isn't simply to get free of the earth and our bodies.

Just as important is the task of bringing love and healing *into* the physical world. We're here to redeem the earth and our bodies—our very humanness.

Christ took on a body—and "experienced all those turmoils, strifes, desires, urges that may be the lot of man in the earth"—not to show kindly sympathy but to honor and recognize high purpose in being human. Or, as Cayce put it in other readings about the purpose of life, we're here *to make the Infinite finite*—to bring the qualities of the spirit into individual form.

Cayce's overall Christology and his interpretation of the Easter story emphasize the living, contemporary quality of Christ's involvement with us. The crucifixion wasn't merely an event one Friday about two thousand years ago. It's also something that unfortunately can go on inside of us each and even day.

By selfishness, fear, and doubt we "crucify Him" in our mind and activities. But just as surely the resurrection is before us every day. His Resurrected Presence is near at hand. "For He, thy Christ, is oft with thee."

Finally, it's important to note a word that Cayce used near the beginning of this reading about Easter and then again near the end. The word is "rededication," and it's the response that Easter invites of us. Easter is about refocusing and recommitting ourselves to what we believe. The message of Easter resanctifies and reconsecrates our humanness. It provides a season—just when the earth is coming back to life in springtime—to devote ourselves again to what our hearts are telling us to do with His promises. We would all do well this Easter season to find time for that kind of rededication.

THE READING

This psychic reading, 5749-6, was given by Edgar Cayce on April 5, 1936. The conductor was Gertrude Cayce.

[1]GC: As we approach this Easter season our thoughts turn naturally toward the biblical accounts of the resurrection of Jesus, the Christ. We seek at this time through this channel information dealing either with a completion of the historical account or interpretation and explanation of the full meaning of the resurrection which will help us to better understand and appreciate it.

[2]EC: Yes. In seeking ye shall find. In the experience of each soul that has named the name of the Christ, this should be a season of rededication of self as being a true messenger of His in and among men.

[3]In seeking, then, to know more of that, as to those here, much may be revealed to those that in their inner selves experienced that material period when *He*, Jesus, walked in the earth.

⁴But for what purpose is this season observed, that caused or called for such a sacrifice that life might be made manifest? Is it not fitting that to those here, to those there in that land, it came at that particular season when life in its manifestations was being demonstrated in the material things about each soul?

⁵How, why, was there the need for there to be a resurrection? Why came He into the earth to die the death, even on the cross? Has it been, then, the fulfillment of promise, the fulfillment of law, the fulfillment of man's estate? Else why did He put on flesh and come into the earth in the form of man, but to be one with the Father; to show to man *his* (man's) divinity, man's relationship to the Maker; to show man that indeed the Father meant it when He said, "If ye call I will hear. Even though ye be far away, even though ye be covered with sin, if ye be washed in the blood of the lamb ye may come back."

⁶Then, though He were the first of man, the first of the sons of God in spirit, in flesh, it became necessary that He fulfill *all* those associations, those connections that were to wipe away in the experience of man that which separates him from his Maker.

⁷Though man be far afield, then, though he may have erred, there is established that which makes for a closer, closer walk *with* Him, through that one who experienced all those turmoils, strifes, desires, urges that may be the lot of man in the earth. Yet He put on flesh, made *Himself* as naught—even as was promised throughout, to those who walked and talked with God.

⁸In the history, then, of the resurrection as ye have recorded in part, may it be so interpreted that those here, now, that experienced (through that period of their advent) His suffering, may—as Andrew, Martha, Naomi, Loda [?], Elois [?], Phoenix [?], Phoebe [?]—again see those days. Though there were fears from the elements without, from the political powers that made for fears of

body and mind, there were the rememberings that *He* had given, "Though ye destroy this temple, in three days it will rise again."

⁹And then as He hung upon the cross, He called to those that He loved and remembered not only their spiritual purposes but their material lives. For He indeed in suffering the death on the cross became the whole, the entire way; *the* way, *the* life, *the* understanding, that we who believe on Him may, too, have the everlasting life. For He committed unto those of His brethren not only the care of the spiritual life of the world but the material life of those that were of his own flesh, his own blood. Yea, as He gave His physical blood that doubt and fear might be banished, so He overcame death; not only in the physical body but in the *spirit* body—that it may become as *one* with Him, even as on that resurrection morn—that ye call thy Eastertide.

¹⁰It is that breaking forth from the tomb, as exemplified in the bulb of the tree of nature itself breaking forth from the sleep that it may rise as He with healing in its very life, to bring all phases of man's experience to His consciousness—that indeed became then the fulfilling of the law.

¹¹On what wise, then, ye ask, did this happen in materiality? Not only was He dead in body, but the soul was separated from that body. As all phases of man in the earth are made manifest, the physical body, the mental body, the soul body became as each dependent upon their own experience. Is it any wonder that the man cried, "My God, my God, *why* hast thou forsaken me?"

¹²Each soul comes to stand as He before that throne of his Maker, with the deeds that have been done in the body, in the mind, presenting the body-spiritual before that throne of mercy, before that throne of the Maker, the Creator, the God.

¹³Yet as He, the Father, hath given to each of you, "I

have given my angels charge concerning thee, and they shall bear thee up, and thou shalt not know corruption."

¹⁴This He demonstrated in the experience of thy Brother, thy Savior, thy Jesus, thy Christ; that would come and dwell in the hearts and lives of you all—if you will but let Him, if you will but invite Him, if you will but open thy own heart, each of you, that He may enter and abide with you.

¹⁵Hence when those of His loved ones and those of His brethren came on that glad morning when the tidings had come to them, those that stood guard heard a fearful noise and saw a light, and—"the stone has been rolled away!" Then they entered into the garden, and there Mary first saw her *risen* Lord. Then came they of His brethren with the faithful women, those that loved His mother, those that were her companions in sorrow, those that were making preparations that the law might be kept that even there might be no desecration of the ground about His tomb. They, too, of His friends, His loved ones, His brethren, saw the angels.

¹⁶How, why, took they on form? That there might be implanted into their hearts and souls that *fulfillment* of those promises.

¹⁷What separates ye from seeing the glory even of Him that walks with thee oft in the touch of a loving hand, in the voice of those that would comfort and cheer? For He, thy Christ, is oft with thee.

¹⁸Doubt, fear, unbelief; fear that thou art not worthy!

¹⁹Open thine eyes and behold the glory, even of thy Christ present here, now, in thy midst! even as He appeared to them on that day!

²⁰What meaneth the story of the Christ, of His resurrection, of the man Jesus that walked in Galilee, without that resurrection morn?

²¹Little, more than that of the man thou thinkest so little of, that though his body-physical touched the bones of

Elisha he walked again among men!

[22]Dost thou believe that He has risen? How spoke Thomas? "Until I see, until I have put my hand in his side where I saw water and blood gush forth, until I have handled his body, I will *not* believe."

[23]Ye, too, oft doubt; ye, too, oft fear. Yet He is surely with thee. And when ye at this glad season rededicate thy life, thy body, thy mind to His service, ye—too—may know, as they, that He *lives*—and is at the right hand of God to make intercession for *you*—if ye will believe; if ye will believe that He is, ye may experience. For as many as have named the name, and that do unto their brethren the deeds that bring to them (to you) that closeness, oneness of purpose with Him, may know—ye, too—in body, in mind, that He *lives today,* and will come and receive you unto Himself, that where He is there ye may be also.

[24]Crucify Him not in thy mind nor in thy bodily activities. Be not overcome by those things that are of the earth-earthy. Rather clothe thy body, thy mind, with the thoughts, the deeds, the privileges that His suffering as a man brought to thee, that He indeed might be the first of those that slept, the first of those that came in the flesh, that passed through all those periods of preparation in the flesh, even as thou.

[25]But if ye would put on Him, ye must claim His promises as thine own. And how canst thou claim them unless ye in thine own knowledge, thine own consciousness, *have* done—do do from day to day—that thy heart has told and does tell thee is in keeping with what He has promised?

[26]For thy Christ, thy Lord, thy Jesus, is nigh unto thee—just now!

[27]We are through.

Chapter 14

A Closer Walk

READING 5758-1

It was the last Christmastime for which Edgar Cayce gave readings—December 1943. His work was so well known by then that he was overwhelmed with requests, and on December 21 he busied himself with five separate readings, three more than his own spiritual advice had recommended.

One of those readings 5758-1, stands as perhaps his finest statement ever about the constant availability of the universal Christ Spirit to each and every one of us. No doubt the quality of this reading was enhanced by the receptivity and spiritual attunement of the people to whom it was given—a local Methodist church group (the Spiritual Life Group) led by longtime Cayce supporter Florence Edmonds. Even the personal messages Cayce gave at the end of the reading to the nine individual group members are inspiring affirmations for us today.

One remarkable feature concerns *spiritual group dynamics* and the psychological terms *personality* and *individuality*. In other Cayce readings (see Chapter 5) the personality is defined as that side of oneself that is shown to the world. It's the familiar self and the one that other people see us to be—somewhat like the "persona," as Carl Jung called it. In contrast, each of us has an individuality which is our more authentic being, even though we may be relatively out of touch with it. That individuality is still in the process of growth and development (i.e., it's not perfect yet).

Paragraph 3 refers to the way in which a group can take on an individuality—what we might refer to as a group consciousness. Although surely any collection of people can develop some sort of group consciousness, how can this take place in the very best way—*what makes it possible for the Christ Consciousness to become the group's collective awareness?* Simply this: It can happen as each member of the group follows the pattern of personality demonstrated by Jesus (for example, through tolerance and forgiveness, as emphasized in paragraphs 4 and 5; or humble service, stressed in paragraph 11).

And what is the result of a collection of people with like ideals discovering the Christ as its group consciousness? A power for good. Paragraph 8 promises that it would be felt not just in their church congregation or simply the Norfolk-Virginia Beach community. It would have an impact worldwide. (A few of these nine group members had been present two-and-a-half years earlier at an annual A.R.E. Congress reading where Cayce had promised that the group of sixty-four people present in that moment had the power to affect directly what would happen to America as war drew near.)

This idea of the Christ as the individuality of the group is reminiscent of the teaching of "no-self" in Buddhism—a doctrine that has perhaps been largely misunderstood in the West as a denial of our individuality. Better understood, the Buddha's insight was that none of us has a separate, independent, unchanging identity. We exist in relationship to each other and the world around us. In fact, this is a theme found time and again in the Cayce readings, not just this one reference in reading 5758-1. Even though the Christ Consciousness may be a pattern written separately within each soul, nevertheless it blossoms and manifests only in relationship to others.

Another repeated theme in this Christmastime reading is the image of a closer walk with our Creator. The Cayce readings always remind us of the accessibility of God. We can have a personal relationship with our Creator. And what better time to remember that truth than the holiday season. Maybe the image can even be acted on rather literally. (A favorite Cayce recommendation was "After breakfast work a while, after lunch rest a while, and after dinner walk a mile.") Take a prayerful walk sometime this Christmas season. Dedicate thirty minutes or an hour to a walking meditation in which you invite the Christ Consciousness to speak with you.

But maybe there is more to this image of walking. One can't help but think of the popular aphorism that each of us must "walk our talk." A rough translation says: words are empty unless they are applied. What does that say about this image that Cayce was fond of using? If we have a "closer walk" with God, it's not simply a private retreat but it's also applying in daily life the spiritual knowledge we have.

One additional element of this reading deserves special note—a theme found in paragraphs 5 and 6. Surely any of us who aspire to awaken the universal Christ Consciousness quickly discover our own shortcomings in such efforts. We have small successes, but probably far more failures. We have moments in the day when we really *are* able to be tolerant of someone's idiosyncrasies. We have successful occasions when we are able to let go of a hurtful comment by someone else (which may or may not really have been intended the way we emotionally took it at first).

But no doubt we have just as many times when we fall

short of the best attitudes and responses. In so many difficult relationship and daily-life challenges, the Christ Consciousness seems rather beyond us. But what's the good news we're reminded of in this Christmastime reading? *Trying* counts. The critical factor is making the effort—even when it doesn't seem to be successful very often. Spiritual growth is rooted in right ideal and intention, coupled with sincere will and effort. Personally reconnecting with that spiritual law might well be the best holiday gift we could give ourselves this year.

THE READING

This psychic reading, 5758-1, was given by Edgar Cayce on December 21, 1943. The conductor was Gertrude Cayce.

[1]GC: Now you will have before you the Spiritual Life Group of the Park Place Methodist Church, some of whose members are present in this room, while other members are at their homes. You will give at this time advice and counsel regarding their work, and how they may best express the spirit of Christ in their work; and you will answer questions asked concerning any phase of it.

[2]EC: Yes, we have the group—Spiritual Life Group, Park Place Methodist Church—as a group, as individuals.

[3]In analyzing or giving that which may be helpful for this group, many personalities are to be taken into consideration. This should be the ideal of each member of such a group; that the personality of the Christ Consciousness may be the individuality of each group; also each individual in the group. And as there is the analyzing of the Christ Life, Christ Consciousness, one realizes and finds that the Christ Child was born into the earth as man; one born in due season, in due time, in man's spiri-

tual evolution, that man might have a pattern of the personality and the individuality of God Himself.

⁴Thus as the individuals in such a group read, analyze, study and apply those tenets, those truths that were presented by the Christ, they find that the Christ Consciousness must become an individual and yet a living thing within their own individual consciousnesses. As with Him, He found no fault in others. This should be the first premise, then, of each individual; less and less condemning of others and more and more of self manifesting that love shown by the Father through the Son in the material world; that man, through this pattern, through this picture of God, may become a living example, may walk closer in that way of less condemning.

⁵For as each individual realizes, as these tenets may be analyzed, if God had condemned—what opportunity would there be for man to find his way back to God? Thus each individual must do unto others as he would have his Brother, the Christ, his God, the Father, do unto him; and indeed, then, apply first, last and always His "Forgive, O God, as I forgive others. Find fault in me, O God, as I find fault in my brother." Less and less then of self, more and more of perfect love, without dissimulations, keeping that faith. Know that as there is the activity of self, self can only sow the seed of truth. And it will be to each individual as was indicated to the children of Israel. They entered into the Promised Land not because of their righteousness but because of the love of the Father for those who tried, who *tried* to live the righteousness.

⁶Thus each individual may have the try counted as righteousness; not as an excuse, neither as justification. For ye have been justified once for all, through the Christ Consciousness that ye seek.

⁷Then the life, the purpose of the individual, the members of such a Life Group, should be that they may walk closer to the Christ day by day in every way. For His

promise has been and is ever to each soul, "If ye will open thy mind, thy heart, I will enter, I will abide with thee." Not as a stranger, but as a brother, as a friend.

[8]In this manner may the group as a group become a power for good, a power magnifying and glorifying the Christ Life in the church, in the community, in the nation, in the world. For in this showing of the seed of the spirit ye sow, and God alone may give the increase, God alone may prepare the heart. For eternal life is never earned—it is the gift of God, by the grace of God— through the giving of the life of the Master, Jesus, who became the Christ by overcoming death, hell and the grave, overcoming the world.

[9]Remember as He has given, it must indeed be that offenses come, but woe unto him by whom they come.

[10]Let it never be said, then, of a single member of the group that ye offended the least of any of His little ones.

[11]Think not more highly of thyself than ye ought, nor consider thyself above thy fellow man. For He that is the greatest will be the servant of all. Even as the Master signified in the bathing of the feet, in the breaking of the bread, in the building of the fire, in the preparation of the food; that the weary in body, in mind might be supplied. And then as He gave to that disciple, He requires of everyone, "feed my lambs, feed my sheep." For all have fallen short, yet recognizing in self that of thyself ye can do nothing, but only as the spirit of truth directeth, ye may accomplish much. Then, entertain only the spirit of truth, the purpose of love, the hope of life. For He gave, "I came that ye might have light, life and love, and have all more abundantly."

[12]And when these things are manifested in the mind and the hearts of the individuals of such a group, yea the world will feel the vibrations, yea the glory of the coming of the Lord. For He tarries not—for some, and in His love abide thee always.

[13]Ready for questions.

[14](Q) As I give the name of each individual member of the group, will you please give an individual message: [3466].

(A) Let that mind be within thee as was in the Christ, that gave Himself that others might know God. Do thou likewise.

[15](Q) R. S.

(A) Let grace keep thee. Let mercy and justice direct thee, that the peace which passeth all understanding may be thine in the consciousness of the Christ Presence.

[16](Q) [993].

(A) Let love be without dissimulation. Abhor that which is evil. Cleave to that which is good. Try ye the purposes in each, but know that the Lord liveth and seeks the love, the help of others.

[17](Q) Edna Hainsworth.

(A) Keep thy heart singing. Be not disturbed, nor let fear come in. For perfect love casteth out fear. Keep thy faith in thy Lord, thy Master.

[18](Q) Hattie Trigg.

(A) Come! Make a joyful noise unto the Lord, Who is thy salvation. Come! Keep thy promises as ye hope that He will keep His promises to thee. Let not doubt nor fear enter, but trust in the Lord.

[19](Q) [2990].

(A) Of him that hath much, much is required. Be not overzealous nor yet overanxious. For the Lord is in His Holy Temple. Prepare that Temple in thine own body, mind and heart, that He may dwell there—ever.

[20](Q) [3377].

(A) Keep the way of the Christ ever before thee in thy uprisings, in thy downsettings. For the Lord hath need of thee today in the hearts of many who look to thee for direction. Let thy life, thy conversations, ever point the way to Christ.

²¹(Q) [3374].

(A) Grace and love are virtues in thee. Keep them in such ways and manners that thy life may direct others, though ye speak never a word. For what the body-mind is speaks louder than what people say. Keep the faith.

²²(Q) [3416].

(A) In the Lord's house are many mansions. In thy mind and heart are many possibilities, many opportunities. Lose not a single one to make known the love that the Master has for the children of men. For He, too, was one of them. So in thy ways of grace and mercy, show forth the Lord's death, the Lord's life, the Lord's love, until He comes again.

²³(Q) May we have a Christmas message from the Master at this time?

(A) Let not your hearts be troubled, neither let them be afraid. For the Lord is in the Holy Temple—let the earth and those that love the Lord rejoice, that the Father-God in the Christ is mindful of men, and He will not let thy loved ones—nor those with and for whom ye pray—be tempted beyond that they are able to bear. But live daily as ye pray, and pray as ye would have thy Brother, the Christ, to praise thy life before the throne of mercy. Show ye mercy and love one to another, then, if ye would have love and mercy shown to thee. For this is the beginning and the end of wisdom.

²⁴We are through.

Chapter 15

THE SECOND COMING

READING 5749-5

The return of Christ is perhaps the most significant of all the prophecies made in the Cayce readings. It was a topic of deep personal interest to Edgar Cayce the man, too. This reading was given to help him prepare material for a scheduled lecture on this subject.

Of course, the Cayce readings are hardly alone in looking for such a great event. "Many . . . have preached concerning this Second Coming." What is special about this reading are some of its themes about the meaning of Christ's return.

Note the unusual way this reading begins. Paragraphs 2-6 serve as an introduction of Cayce, like a master of ceremonies making preparatory comments before bringing on-stage the scheduled speaker. It's unclear who or what this introducer is—some other aspect of Cayce's own soul, another spiritual being momentarily speaking through the entranced Cayce's body, or something else? In that "introduction" is a remarkable label for Cayce and his work: "forerunner of . . . the Christ Consciousness." We might presume that this refers both to the teachings found in the readings themselves and to the clairvoyant sensitivity that Cayce demonstrated.

Also mentioned in the introduction is Cayce's visionary dream. It came during another reading that very morning. (There are many examples of this phenomenon in which one aspect of Cayce's mind is giving a reading while another aspect is dreaming.) In the dream he was on a luxurious train with white and gold interior. Traveling with him were several famous evangelists, each of them deceased. They were headed to a spot where John, the Beloved Disciple, would be teaching. Cayce asked one of the evangelists if he remembered Cayce. The evangelist replied—apparently as a symbolic reference to Cayce still being alive in the physical world—"Oh yes, but you are not just like we are . . . You are on this same train with us right now, but don't forget you have to go back and don't you get too far away." As paragraph 4 points out, this visionary dream was directly related to Cayce's concerns about the meaning of the Second Coming.

The heart of this reading then begins with paragraph 7, which contains many of the central elements of Cayce's theological position about Christ. For example, Christ is the first to conquer death (i.e., to "put on immortality"). Christ came not to judge and condemn us—since we are already self-condemning in our willfulness and separation from God.

As if to answer definitively the question of Christ's possible return, paragraph 7 ends with a theme that is echoed in paragraph 12. Christ has come and will come in any age when there is need. In human evolution, there have been windows of opportunity—periods of possible breakthrough. He manifests directly in human affairs whenever we are ready for a new level of understanding and application of *one basic principle:* Our Creator is Spirit and any worshipful approach to that Creator must be a spiritual one based on right understanding and truth.

In this reading Cayce presents a *broad* view of Christ

as one who has been intimately involved in human evolution for many millennia. Instead of a single remarkable visit to earth 2,000 years ago, Cayce's Christology describes Him as a guide and sustainer of longstanding. In this light, we might be more accurate in wondering about "another coming" instead of merely a "Second Coming." With each return humanity is nudged back toward the divine plan for spiritual evolution—what Cayce refers to here as "continued activity toward the proper understanding and proper relationships . . . [to] Him . . ."

Christ and His influence have been experienced in different ways in different time periods. Not always has it been a direct incarnation, although in both paragraphs 15 and 16 there are clear references to the possibility of His coming again "in body" and "in the flesh." But sometimes it has been His Spirit inspiring and directing men and women who have served as leaders to their people. The work of such individuals is bound to cause upset to people whose values and ideals are rooted in materialism (i.e., "contention in the minds and hearts of those that dwell in the flesh"). That Christ impulse always operates to counteract the forces of hate, prejudice, selfishness, and the other shortcomings listed in paragraph 14.

We might well ask ourselves two questions in regard to the possibility of another coming of Christ. First, are we in a period of human history that is ripe for the Christ influence to engage us directly once again? That is, are we ready for a breakthrough—a quantum jump to some new application of that one, central principle? Many would argue yes and point to certain promising signs—evidence of a potential meeting place for science and spirituality. The convergence of science and religion would certainly be a breakthrough for humanity. Another hopeful sign—in the spirit of oneness—is the ecumenical vision of many religious leaders. This spirit provides deep appreciation and respect for the value and truth in all traditions of faith—another possible breakthrough that qualifies for a new application of the central principle.

Second, we might ask ourselves what each of us individuals can do in order to make that return possible. This is not the only reading in which Cayce makes clear that preparatory work was done in advance of Christ's coming two thousand years ago. What's more, it would be needed just as much in today's world. The hopeful possibility of Christ's return becomes a reality only "as there is prepared the way by those that have made and do make the channels for the entering in . . . " It's in the little acts of kindness and tolerance that each of us can play a big role.

THE READING

This psychic reading, 5749-5, was given by Edgar Cayce on May 1, 1934. The conductor was Gertrude Cayce.

[1]GC: You will have before you Edgar Cayce, present in this room, and his inquiring mind in relation to the talk which he expects to give next Monday evening on the "Second Coming." You will give what he should present at this open meeting on this subject.

[2]EC: That which crowds in at the present may be well for those present, but would it be well for those in open meeting? From this experience, though, there may be gathered that which has been given and that which may be helpful to many in the comprehension of that which is the experience of those that seek through such channels to have for themselves the experience that may be had by those here in this room in the present.

[3]Be mindful then, each of you, of that ye may inwardly

experience in that which may be given you.

⁴For, those experiences that have been told you of the vision [E.C.'s dream of that a.m.] of the gathering of those that were known to many in this present land and in the lands abroad were in reference to just those things that may be said respecting the Coming.

⁵Many of these have ministered, have preached concerning this Second Coming. Not a one but what has at some time left the record of his contemplations and experiences in those environs, whether made in the heart and mind of his hearers or in the written word; yet here today, in what ye call time, ye find them gathering in a body to *listen* to that as may be given them by [Edgar Cayce?] one who is to be a forerunner of that influence in the earth known as the Christ Consciousness, the coming of that force or power into the earth that has been spoken of through the ages.

⁶Listen, while he speaks! [Edgar Cayce?]

⁷Ye, my brethren, in your ignorance and in your zeal have often spoken of that influence in the earth known among men as the record made by those that would influence the activities in the religious or spiritual life of individuals through the ages, as a record of the Son of man as He walked in the earth. Rather would ye listen and harken to those things as He spoke when He made those inferences and illustrations as to how those had closed and did close their ears to what was actually going on about them; yet they knew Him not! He, our Lord and our Master, was the first among those that put on immortality that there might be the opportunity for those forces that had erred in spiritual things; and only through experiencing in a manner whereunto all might be visioned from their greater abilities of manifesting in the various phases, forms and manners as they developed through that ye know as matter, could they come to know how or why or when there was made manifest

in any realm spirit that was good and spirit that was in error. For, He gave thee, had ye not *known* the Son ye would *not* be condemned in thine own self. For, condemnation was not in Him, but "ye are condemned already." And in the coming into the influence of those that would open themselves for an understanding might there be the approach to Him. He has come in all ages through those that were the spokesmen to a people in this age, that age, called unto a purpose for the manifestation of that first idea.

[8]Readst thou how the sons of God came together, and Satan came also? "Hast thou considered my servant? Hast thou seen his ways?" And the answer, even from the evil force, "Put forth thine hand—touch him in those things that pertain to the satisfying of desire that is flesh, and he will curse thee to thy face." Then, "He is in thine hand, but touch not his soul—touch not his soul!"

[9]So we see how that the coming into the earth has been and is for the evolution or the evolving of the soul unto its awareness of the effect of all influences in its experience in the varied spheres of activity; and that only in Him who was the creator, the maker, the experiencer of mortality and spirit and soul *could* this be overcome.

[10]Then, the necessity. For, has it not been said, has it not been shown in the experience of the earth, the world, from any angle it may be considered, that He has not willed that any should be lost—but has prepared the way of escape in Him, the Maker?

[11]But who is the worthy servant? He that has endured unto the end!

[12]Then, He has come in all ages when it has been necessary for the understanding to be centered in a *new* application of the same thought, "God *is* Spirit and seeks such to worship him in spirit and in truth!"

[13]Then, as there is prepared the way by those that have made and do make the channels for the entering in,

there may come into the earth those influences that will save, regenerate, resuscitate, *hold*—if you please—the earth in its continued activity toward the proper understanding and proper relationships to that which is the making for the closer relationships to that which is in Him *alone*. Ye have seen it in Adam; ye have heard it in Enoch, ye have had it made known in Melchizedek; Joshua, Joseph, David, and those that made the preparation then for him called Jesus. Ye have seen His Spirit in the leaders in all realms of activity, whether in the isles of the sea, the wilderness, the mountain, or in the various activities of every race, every color, every activity of that which has produced and does produce contention in the minds and hearts of those that dwell in the flesh.

[14]For, what must be obliterated? Hate, prejudice, selfishness, backbiting, unkindness, anger, passion, and those things of the mire that are created in the activities of the sons of men.

[15]Then again He may come in body to claim His own. Is He abroad today in the earth? Yea, in those that cry unto Him from every corner; for He, the Father, hath not suffered His soul to see corruption; neither hath it taken hold on those things that make the soul afraid. For, He *is* the Son of Light, of God, and is holy before Him. And He comes again in the hearts and souls and minds of those that seek to know His ways.

[16]These be hard to be understood by those in the flesh, where prejudice, avarice, vice of all natures holds sway in the flesh; yet those that call on Him will not go emptyhanded—even as thou, in thine ignorance, in thine zealousness that has at times eaten thee up. Yet *here* ye may hear the golden scepter ring—ring—in the hearts of those that seek His face. Ye, too, may minister in those days when He will come in the flesh, in the earth, to call His own by name.

[17]We are through.

The *A.R.E. Membership Series*

This book continues a series that is published by the Association for Research and Enlightenment, Inc., for individuals who are especially interested in their personal and spiritual growth and transformation.

The A.R.E. was founded in 1931 as a nonprofit organization to study, research, and disseminate information on ESP, dreams, holistic health, meditation, and life after death. The A.R.E. continues its mission today, nurturing a worldwide membership with conferences, study groups, and a variety of publications—all aimed at helping seekers find paths that will lead to a more fulfilling life, mentally, physically, and spiritually. The hallmark of A.R.E.'s publications is to be helpful and hopeful. A.R.E. is committed to assisting in personal growth and making available nourishing entertainment.

Many of the books published by A.R.E. are available in bookstores throughout the world and all are available directly from the A.R.E.'s mail-order catalogs.

Three new books in this *A.R.E. Membership Series* are sent at no cost each year to individuals who are Sponsoring members or Life members of A.R.E. Each of the titles in this series will become available, one year after initial publication, for purchase by individuals throughout the world who are interested in individual growth and transformation.

For more information about membership benefits of the nonprofit Association for Research and Enlightenment, Inc., please see the next page.

You Can Receive Books Like This One
and Much, Much More

You can begin to receive books in the *A.R.E. Membership Series* and many more benefits by joining the nonprofit Association for Research and Enlightenment, Inc., as a Sponsoring or Life member.

The A.R.E. has a worldwide membership that receives a wide variety of study aids, all aimed at assisting individuals in their spiritual, mental, and physical growth.

Every member of A.R.E. receives a copy of *Venture Inward*, the organization's bimonthly magazine; an in-depth topical newsletter on alternate months; opportunity to borrow, through the mail, from a collection of more than 400 files on medical and metaphysical subjects; access to one of the world's most complete libraries on metaphysical and spiritual subjects; and opportunities to participate in conferences, international tours, a retreat-camp for children and adults, and numerous nationwide volunteer activities.

In addition to the foregoing benefits, Sponsoring and Life members also receive at no charge three books each year in the *A.R.E. Membership Series.*

If you are interested in finding out more about membership in A.R.E. and the many benefits that can assist you on your path to fulfillment, you can easily contact the Membership Department by writing Membership, A.R.E., P.O. Box 595, Virginia Beach, VA 23451-0595 or by calling **1-800-333-4499** or faxing **1-804-422-4631**.